Rock Bottom is Where

Bad Bitches are Built:

Find Your Footing; Conquer the Climb

Dr. Erica L. Adkins

Paperback ISBN: 978-1-7365161-0-2
eBook ISBN: 978-1-7365161-1-9
Hardcover ISBN: 978-1-7365161-2-6

Get Your Free Gift!

To get the best experience with this book, I've found readers who download and use the *Rock Bottom is Where Bad Bitches Are Built Workbook* are able to implement the concepts faster and take the next steps needed to heal.

You can get a copy by visiting:
www.drericaadkins.com/rockbottom

Note

For Conner, Avery, and Amaya

Table of Contents

Introduction

Rock bottom. The lowest possible point. Rock bottom can be described as a time when an individual believes things cannot get any worse for them. I can think of quite a few instances in my life where I've had the thought, "this is it. This MUST be rock bottom" only to have something worse come along.

During one particularly awful event, I said to my best friend, "I don't know how much more of this I can take. I feel like I am always being kicked when I'm down." Her response to me was, "Erica, rock bottom is where bad bitches are built."

The wisdom in her words reminded me that I had trudged through pain, trauma, heartbreak, healing, more pain, more trauma, and not only lived to tell the tale, but came out on top time and time again. Rising to the top following a traumatic event is not something that comes easily. It takes hard work. It takes perseverance. It takes putting one foot in front of the other. It takes just breathing sometimes.

It began as a freshman at Denison University, I felt "different" from the moment I stepped onto the campus. The parking lot was full of BMWs and fancy SUVs. Students were dressed in clothes I could never imagine being able to afford. My high school principal had warned me that I might not fit in there. I of course set out to prove him wrong, because at 18 years old, I knew everything. He was right. It wasn't the place for me. I met many great friends and wonderful professors. The experience wasn't negative overall, but it wasn't for me. While I was a student there, I experienced sadness and emptiness on a level I had not experienced before. I shared my sadness with a close friend and shared some things about myself that I had only shared with one other individual in middle school. She encouraged me to seek treatment at our counseling center.

There, I met Dr. Jeffry Pollard, a licensed psychologist. Dr. Pollard sat with me. He held my grief and was present and attentive. He metaphorically took my hand and led me to the start of the path of healing. I remember sitting in his office during my first visit. He had stepped into another room to grab some paperwork, and I was admiring his diplomas and degrees on the wall. I thought to myself, "wow! How great would it be to be a psychologist? But I'm not smart enough to do that". Words from a high school mentor/teacher echoed in my head, "Erica you should go straight through and get your Ph.D." my response "But I'm not smart enough to do that." Dr. Pollard helped me to heal, and also helped me by encouraging me to follow my dreams, and by telling me I was smart enough to do whatever I set out to do.

Decades later, I share the same credentials as Dr. Pollard, and I share the same love and compassion for every person I encounter. Over time, I've learned you don't always know the purpose of the path you are on until you reach your final destination, or until something along the way makes it make sense. I know my purpose in life is to help people heal from wounds of trauma.

Recovering from trauma is difficult. Trauma often goes hand in hand with shame, fear, self-loathing, depression, anxiety, etc. Not only am I educated and trained on how to help individuals, families, and communities heal from trauma, but I am a survivor as well. I have experienced childhood trauma, infidelity, suicide of several close individuals, domestic violence, single parenting during moments when I was struggling to survive, Post-Traumatic Stress Disorder (PTSD), deployment, a chronic debilitating illness, and an unthinkable trauma happening to one of my daughters.

As a licensed psychologist, my job is to sit with people during their darkest moments, help them find the light, and help them heal the broken parts of themselves. I help them find the courage to keep going - to put one foot in front of the other. In the pages that follow, I want to take you on the journey of my life. Of my pain. I want to show you that pain and trauma can happen to anyone and that you can not only HEAL but you can GROW and THRIVE following horrific incidents.

Is it easy? No. Will it hurt? Hell yes. Do you have to do it alone? Absolutely not. I will show you that you have what it takes to rise above. That when you feel as if you have hit rock bottom and cannot possibly move forward, that is just the beginning, brave and courageous one. This book will be the metaphorical hand reaching down to rock bottom and pulling you back up again so you can continue your journey. After all, rock bottom is where bad bitches are built, so let's get to work!

Chapter One:
Rock Bottom

On Easter Sunday, March 31, 2013, I was alone with my children. That day, I opened Facebook on my laptop, something I typically only did on my smartphone. I noticed a message in a category that I could not see on my phone, a tab for messages from people you are not friends with. "Hmm . . . that's strange," I thought to myself. For whatever reason, on that particular Sunday, at that particular moment, I read that message.

As soon as I opened it, my heart began to race and pound in my chest. My hands shook and my palms began to sweat. The room spun and turned dark, as if I were about to pass out. There was a picture of a brand-new baby boy with a message from a woman I had never heard of telling me that my husband had had an affair with her, his ex, and that they had a third son together.

My world stopped at that moment. Everything I thought I knew about my life and my marriage suddenly seemed like a lie. To make the situation more unsettling, I was 16 weeks pregnant with my youngest child. There I was, alone on Easter Sunday with my 9- and 6-year-old, pregnant, devastated, and unable to move.

When the room stopped spinning momentarily, I grabbed my laptop and ran to my room. I kept telling myself, "just breathe," "just get upstairs," "don't let the kids see you are upset." I collapsed on the floor next to my bed and called my best friend. For what seemed like hours, she stayed on the phone with me. She talked me through my next steps. She reassured me that no matter what, I would be okay.

The following morning, I got up and went to work. I didn't skip a beat. Routine was all that was holding me together. After dropping the kids off at school, I had an hour's drive to work to contemplate how the hell I was going to make it through the day.

Working at a prison is never easy. Working as a female psychologist at a Special Management Unit in a United States Penitentiary as about as far from easy as you might imagine. Walking into work that morning, I felt like I was in a tunnel. My vision was blurry and sounds seemed muffled. "Breathe, Erica. Just breathe. Just put one foot in front of the other." Collecting my keys and radio from the control center and heading to my office, I contemplated telling my coworkers what had happened. I had only worked there for a month. I was the new girl, still trying to find my place in the department and earn the trust of my coworkers. The thought of sharing one of the most hurtful, vulnerable moments of my life with people I barely knew but wanted desperately to connect with seemed like too much.

Going over my mental "to-do" list, I thought of the items that had to be completed that day, and things that could wait. Of course, on any day working with that population you could expect several inmates would require suicide risk assessments or behavioral intervention. That day I prayed to God "please, please God, spare me today. I do not have what it takes to walk into that unit and deal with that mess. Not today, God." God did not listen, or perhaps God listened, and knew that if anyone could handle these challenges, it was me.

Shortly after sitting down at my desk and opening my email, I hear, "Bravo A to psychology, Dr. Adkins," my heart sank. "Go for Adkins," I said while keying the mic on my radio. "What's your phone 20?" I give my number over the radio and soon receive a call from the BA Officer in Charge.

"Hey doc, inmate Jones is refusing to give up the law library. He says he's suicidal and needs to see you." Inmate Jones was a known entity to us. Similar to many of his fellow inmates on the unit, he had a personality disorder and often engaged in self-injurious behavior. At times he had legitimate mental health concerns. Often, he was either bored and wanted something to entertain himself or was pissed off over some perceived injustice and stated he was suicidal in order for someone to negotiate with him. "Roger. I'm in route."

The walk from my office to BA felt like running a gauntlet of imaginary foes while taking hits from both sides. The recreation yard was empty, yet I felt a million eyes on me as I walked. I imagined everyone that looked at me knew, knew the pain of what I was going through. The shame. The fear. The worry. The rage. Knew that each step I took was a tremendous feat in and of itself. Each breath I took was measured and calculated. Breathe in (two, three, four), hold (two, three, four), breathe out (two, three, four) hold (two, three, four).

Finally, I arrived at the door. "Psychology to bravo A at your door." I keyed the mic on my radio to alert the staff to come unlock the door for me. Entering the unit, I immediately heard inmate Jones yelling from the tiny cage designated as the "law library" in the middle of the tier. I walked over to him, careful to position myself between the officer's station and the law library cage so as not to be seen by the other inmates as most of them peered through the tiny window in their cell door, hoping for a glimpse of a female.

As I attempted to listen to inmate Jones recount the latest perceived injustice, I suddenly felt the room start to spin. Everything got dark and all I could hear was a very loud buzzing in my ears. "Your husband had a baby with another woman. Your husband had a baby with another woman," echoing through my head over, and over, and over. I heard nothing inmate Jones was saying to me, yet still managed the appropriate head nod and verbal affirmations "uh huh" "yeah" showing that I was "listening" to him.

Suddenly he stopped. "Dr. Adkins you alright? You don't look so good." I reassured him I was fine, but that I'm a little under the weather and could we try our best to wrap this up as quickly as possible. For once in his life, he showed some mercy. "Yeah. I got you, doc. I'll go back to my cell now. When you gonna come see me again?" I agreed to speak to him during rounds later in the week and promised to bring him some reading material.

As quickly as possible, I raced into the officer's station and collapsed in a chair. The lieutenant knew I was pregnant, but had no idea what took place with my husband. He offered to let me out the back door of the unit to avoid being seen by other inmates.

Escaping out the back door of the unit and heading back to my office, I finally exhaled. Walking to my office, I slowed my steps. "One foot in front of the other, Erica. That's all you have to do. Put one foot in front of the other." That day, standing in the middle of that unit listening to inmate Jones, I thought, "surely this must be rock bottom."

Climbing from rock bottom

This book is not your traditional "self-help" book. It is not written by an expert who may or may not have struggled with problems they are telling you how to fix. This book is written by a psychologist. A person with the training, knowledge, skills, abilities, and clinical experiences that lend itself to helping people heal. But this book is also written by an average human being that has had to overcome extraordinary circumstances and traumas. My goal is to lead you and show you the way by sharing my story and sharing what helped me. I hope you haven't experienced your husband having a baby with another woman while you were pregnant with his child. But chances are you have a "rock bottom" story of your own. Don't hide it. Telling your story can set you free. Telling your story can remind you how strong you are and what you have overcome. I'll share with you some "footholds" that helped me get back on my feet.

When working through trauma history, I use the metaphor of climbing Mount Everest. You cannot wake up one morning and climb all the way to the top in one day with no gear, no preparation, no trail guide to lead the way. Instead, you might take the time to research what you need, ways to best train and prepare. You may even hire a trail guide that is familiar and has completed the hike before you. You might feel inspired by talking to others who have hiked Mount Everest or reading stories of their triumphs and successes. Healing from trauma is very similar. It is a journey, a process, a non-linear path. Together we are hiking Mount Everest. I cannot do the work for you, just as no one did the work for me. You have to carry your pack and traverse the tough areas. However, I will be right by your side, just as my guides were, guiding you and giving you direction about parts of the trail that are difficult and what to expect as we move ahead. Trail guides and experienced climbers can guide you by pointing out solid "footholds" or places to put your feet in order to regain balance or footing.

Trauma and shame often go hand in hand. We are taught along the way that bad things happen to us because we are bad. No! This is not true! Bad things happen to us because bad things happen. You are not what has happened to you. You are so much more than that. You do not have to continue to suffer for eternity and carry around the burden of your trauma as punishment. You deserve to heal. You deserve to rise above stronger than ever.

Footholds

Friendship. In this situation and many others that follow, my best friend(s) were pillars of strength and were my trail guides on the climb from rock bottom. They allowed me to lean on them, and they gave me a boost when I felt I couldn't do it on my own. From this experience, I learned I was so much stronger than I thought I was. Look around you. There are women who have done hard things and survived hard things. You are one of those women. Reach out to friends and family and ask for what you need. If you don't have friends and family that you trust, or that are safe, reach out to a professional or to a support group. Great healing can be found by sharing your story with others that have experienced similar hardships. Great wisdom can be found in hearing their stories as well.

Will. The will to survive was strong. I recognized that the only way around this pain was to go through it. To move forward. I willed myself to put one foot in front of the other. The old saying "where there is a will there is a way" holds a great deal of truth. After I found out about my husband's son, I had no choice but to move forward. My mantra became "just put one foot in front of the other Erica. One foot in front of the other". When you feel as if you cannot go on, that you cannot possibly come back from a rock bottom moment, remember what you are made of. Will yourself to get up, get moving, and put one foot in front of the other.

Breath: Returning to our basic life source, our breath, can help to calm and center us. Just breathe. Sometimes that is the best you can do. Just breathe. Focus inward on the feeling of your breath moving in and out of your lungs. If you can feel the breath moving in and out, it means you are still alive, and that time is still moving forward. With each breath you take, and each step forward, you are moving in the right direction. No matter what tough situation you are facing, you can continue to breathe.

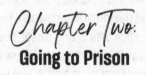

Chapter Two:
Going to Prison

Let's rewind the clock a bit.

In 2004, I was a doctoral student and had just had a baby. I was battling postpartum depression and questioning my entire life. I wasn't sure if I needed a Ph.D. and wasn't sure what the heck I wanted to do with my life. While working at a local community college as a counselor and academic advisor, I noticed a pattern of men coming in and seeking advice on what career fields were open to them with a felony record.

On one particular day, a gentleman came into my office in the prison release uniform of a white t-shirt and khaki pants. He had his belongings in a paper bag, having come directly from the bus station after being released. He was determined to do better and make something of his life. When asked, "what careers are open to me?" I began to see the barriers individuals with felony records faced when trying to better their lives. This sent me on a search to learn more.

In doing so, I discovered the Federal Bureau of Prisons offered a pre-doctoral internship program for psychology students at approximately 10 prisons throughout the United States. From that moment on, I dedicated myself to returning to school and finishing my doctoral degree. Every research paper I wrote, every clinical experience I sought out was somehow linked to incarceration in order to learn as much as possible and make myself competitive for the internship program.

After several years and a lengthy application and interview process, I matched with my top internship site. In August of 2008, I moved my 4-year-old son, 2-year-old daughter, and husband to Fort Worth, Texas to pursue my dream of becoming a prison psychologist and helping inmates return to society with marketable skill sets and knowledge about the world of work.

Within the first couple of weeks, I noticed the complex politics at play, both amongst staff members and the inmate population. I was happy to be there and eager to prove myself. My office was a tiny closet-sized room in the basement of an old government hospital. It had one tiny window that could not be opened. It was right around the corner from what had at one time been the morgue. Talk about creepy. In addition to the eerie nature of the basement environment, we were constantly battling rats. We'd see their droppings and occasionally see one dart across an office or room. The worst part was when they would die in the ceiling tiles and create the worst smell imaginable.

My first rotation of the year was in correctional psychology. On this rotation, I would make rounds in the Special Housing Unit (SHU) in the jail (our facility had a separate jail facility for pretrial inmates and inmates undergoing forensic evaluations), conduct suicide risk assessments, and respond to any behavioral health crises that arose.

To this day, I still remember the full name and inmate register number of my first suicide risk assessment. This particular inmate became well known to our department, and to myself specifically. He often engaged in self-injurious behavior (such as cutting) and would have to be placed on suicide watch, requiring constant supervision and daily evaluation by a psychologist or intern. On more than one occasion, he would harm himself with any object he could find such as an eating utensil or pencil, while I was standing at his door speaking with him. I remember the fear I felt the first time this occurred, and I had to call for help on the radio. Over time, experiences such as this became the norm and no longer "rattled" me, but as a young intern it was upsetting.

Walked Out

In the Bureau of Prisons, when someone loses their job, we call it being "walked out". The term comes from the fact that once you lose your job, you can no longer be in the prison unescorted, so often you would see a staff member walking across the prison compound with a box of their belongings being escorted by a correctional lieutenant.

During my internship year, I was threatened with being "walked out" four different times. The first time only 2 months into the internship year. I was in my office typing up an assessment when I felt very nauseous. Afraid of being sick, I ran to the bathroom. Once I felt better, I walked back to my office to find one of the drug treatment specialists (DTS) standing in front of my open office door. This might not seem like a big deal, but in a prison, you can NEVER leave a door unlocked, especially not to an office that has a computer and phone access. I immediately felt sick all over again. I asked the DTS if she had found my door open like that. She said she had. We both agreed she would report it to her supervisor and I would report it as well.

Shortly after speaking to my supervisor, I was called to the Captain's office. The Captain is the head supervisor of all the corrections staff and of the daily institutional operations. The closer I got to his office, the harder I cried. I knew I had made a huge mistake, one worthy of losing my job and internship.

As I walked, I thought about all the ramifications of losing my internship. I would have to move somewhere else, but how could I afford that? It took all of our savings to get to Texas. I would have to apply again for internship the following year and risk not being selected. What if I never graduated? How would I feed my family? My husband was not working at the time, so my income supported the family. All of this went through my mind as I walked down the hallway to his office.

My supervisor and the Chief Psychologist met me in his office. He asked for my side of the story. I explained what had happened, how long the door had been unattended, etc. He was very patient and forgiving. He reiterated the importance of institutional security, and said he was going to use this as a learning experience for me, but would not "walk me out." He let me go back to work.

Very early on, I realized I was not well-liked by several of the other psychologists, including the Chief. I came into internship thinking I had to prove myself. I had to show them I could work independently and function in the capacity of a psychologist. I thought that was what internship was for and what they expected of me. Unfortunately, my drive and desire to "prove" myself came across as me being a "know it all" and being "untrainable."

I learned the hard way that in the Bureau of Prisons (and many other internship environments), interns are at the bottom of the food chain. The expectation is the intern looks up to and admires the psychologists and constantly asks for guidance and approval. Once I realized this, I tried to change how I interacted with the psychologists, but by then it was too late. Below is an excerpt from my journal during that timeframe. I tried very hard to affirm myself and my intentions and to turn negative beliefs and thoughts into positive ones:

September 27th 2008

What a week! Work pretty much sucked. I feel very targeted and feel as if some karmic occurrence was happening. I don't know if I'm cut out for this. The Chief Psychologist told me I need to be more correctionally minded. She said to ask myself at the end of each interaction with the client is there any correctional issue happening here? I'm also going to call Dr. A on Monday and get her perspective and tips on being more correctionally minded. I do want to learn. I also want to be happy with who I am.

I need to allow myself permission to be an intern, and to learn and grow as an intern and other professional. I need to stop trying to function as an independent professional and focus more on being an intern. I am allowed to learn. I am allowed to receive feedback. I am a good person even when I make mistakes. Everyone makes mistakes. There is a meaning in the message and what happened this week. I don't yet know what it is, but it will become clear to me. The good news is this allows me room for improvement. It allows me to work hard at being on my A game and make improvements to the quality of my work. I do want to learn. I do not want a chip on my shoulder. I am a good clinician. I am a good writer. I am scientifically minded. I will be a success because I have many strengths. I will use my strengths to move myself forward. I will work very hard to be more correctionally oriented. I will work to have people know the real me. I will work hard to stay true to the real me. I will work hard to be comfortable with the real me.

My goal has been to get a job with the Bureau of Prisons, but I don't just want a job for a paycheck and some benefits, I want a career where I can make an impact. I want a career where I can be a social change agent, opening peoples' eyes to injustice and inefficiency. I can do this. I can make it through this year a success. I can ask the Training Director if I can help her count on Wednesdays. I will be more interactive with corrections staff on the jail and at the main line. I can do this. I can be a kick @ss intern for sure. I will be an intern the Bureau won't want to lose. I also need to focus on taking better care of myself mentally, physically, emotionally and spiritually.

The second time they threatened me with being walked out was when an inmate I had been working with disclosed to me he feared for his life and had been threatened by other inmates because of his sexual orientation. I took the appropriate steps and notified the lieutenant, and we placed the inmate in protective custody (PC).

While he was being interviewed by one psychologist prior to being placed in PC, he disclosed that he had been being pressured by other inmates in his housing unit for sexual favors. He had previously disclosed to me that other inmates had asked him for sex, but that he declined and did not feel pressured or threatened. The BOP has a very strict policy on the prevention of sexual abuse and rape. The Prison Rape Elimination Act was taken very seriously, and we were all committed to keeping inmates safe and free from sexual trauma or pressure. According to the PREA protocol, when an inmate feels "pressured" for sex, this requires a report and investigation. As an intern, I was learning this policy. The inmate had denied feeling pressured and did not seem bothered by the requests. The psychologist doing his evaluation raised the issue with the chief psychologist, and again I was in danger of losing my job and internship.

I have no problem admitting when I have made a mistake. I try my best to learn from them and do better. My internship was traumatic because of the nature of the environment, and the nature of the climate within the department. There was very little margin of error for me. I was one of four interns, and the only one threatened with being walked out, despite other interns making minor mistakes as well. Fortunately, I was spared again.

The other two times were silly and ultimately inconsequential. Needless to say, I was more than ready for the internship to be over. The incredible amount of pressure and stress I was under from the work environment combined with the difficulty of the work itself took its toll. My marriage was rocky at the start of internship. We had come close to divorce when my oldest was 6 months old, but with a great deal of therapy and commitment to make it work, we stuck it out.

During my internship year, my husband began chiropractic school. I was glad for him and supported him 100%. However, with both of us being under tremendous stress and pressure and raising 2 small children with no family support, our relationship crumbled. We made the difficult decision to separate once the internship was over. We spent several months living in the same space until that time, and decided not to tell the kids that the relationship was ending, just that Mommy was taking a job in Louisiana while Daddy stayed in Texas for school.

The kids and I moved to Louisiana in August of 2009. I spent weekends driving back and forth to Texas so the kids could see their Dad. During this time period, it became clear my marriage was not salvageable. We filed for divorce in January of 2010 and it was final the day before my son turned 6 in March of the same year.

Strangely, the weekend my divorce was final is one of my fondest memories. My ex and I had committed to staying friendly and civil for the kids. I went to court alone on that Friday while he stayed at his apartment with the kids. I spent the weekend staying at his apartment. We took the kids to the Fort Worth Zoo and Chuck E. Cheese for my son's birthday. I remember feeling happy and carefree that weekend while also feeling deep, deep sadness that our marriage had not survived.

That feels like such a long time ago. Sometimes I miss my little family. Looking back, it's painful to remember the level of stress and pressure I felt during that time period. I remember it clearly and vividly. For each step I took forward, it seemed I took 3 back. Every time I fell to what I thought was the lowest point, I would metaphorically get kicked in the face as I was trying to get up. It was a long road.

Climbing from Rock Bottom

So what? What do I want you to take from this story? I want you to know you can do hard things. I learned quite a few lessons throughout my doctoral program and internship. The most powerful lesson being that I can do hard things. You might be determined (or some may say stubborn) like me and vow to prove people wrong when they express doubt about your ability to accomplish something. This has been a trait I've relied on throughout my life to motivate me to get through hard times. The satisfaction of achieving goals you set for yourself is worth the struggle and the sacrifice, regardless of whether anyone else recognizes it.

Footholds

Expectations. Initially I had extremely unrealistic expectations for myself, for my family and for internship. One foothold that helped most was adjusting my expectations to be more realistic. Have realistic expectations for yourself! Are you expecting yourself to be superhuman? To be perfect? To be flawless? For life to always be easy? No one is perfect. Even diamonds aren't flawless, and life is not easy. Adjust your expectations, my friend. Make them realistic and achievable. You will constantly be disappointed in yourself if your expectations are unreasonable. Try asking, "what do I expect of myself? What do I expect of this situation? Follow those up with "are these expectations realistic?"

Self-Compassion:

I try my best to practice self-compassion. Dr. Kristen Neff defines "self-compassion" as giving ourselves the same kindness and care we'd give to a good friend. This practice was new to me. I worked hard to give myself grace and compassion. Pay attention to the voices in your head telling you "you can't do it", that you "aren't good enough", that you "deserve to be hurt or to fail." If your best friend came to you with the same problem, would you say those things to her? If the answer is no, then change how you talk to yourself. Be kind with your words. Be kind to yourself, my dear friend. You deserve it. You are worthy of all the love and compassion you offer to others.

Permission:

I gave myself permission to be human. This was difficult. As I already mentioned, I had very high expectations of myself. I had to give myself permission to feel my feelings. I am giving you the same. You are human! Humans make mistakes. Humans experience trauma. Humans go through hard things, but we can also do hard things. You have my permission to be human and to feel your feelings. No matter what you are feeling, it is valid. As humans, we have a range of emotions and all serve a purpose at one point or another. Our emotions or our feelings are a way for our brain to give us feedback about our situation or our environment. It is more than acceptable to feel and express a broad range of feelings. A question I will often ask myself is "are my feelings matching up with the situation?" Sometimes I feel very big feelings about a minor situation. Sometimes I feel minimal feelings about something "big" or "traumatic". No judgement. Notice your feelings and practice allow them to metaphorically "float" away if they don't seem to match the situation. If it seems your feelings are minimal, ask yourself, "what am I protecting myself from? What am I afraid of?"

Forward Momentum:

One foot in front of the other has been my motto for many years. No matter how hard things are, take a breath and put one foot in front of the other. Each step brings you closer to resolution and healing. Forward march!

Chapter Three:
Disney Monday

Shortly after arriving at USP Pollock, I became the Mental Health Expert on the Crisis Negotiation Team (CNT). In late April/early May of 2010, our team, together with the Special Operations Response Team (SORT), the Crisis Support Team (CST) and the Disturbance Control Team (DCT) headed to Fort Hood Texas to meet up with other crisis response teams from the South-Central Region for training. The morning we left the institution in Louisiana, we stopped briefly at a gas station close to the prison. I remember walking toward the gas pump to grab a napkin as my friend had spilled my coffee in our van.

As I walked toward the gas pump, I saw an officer from SORT walking the same direction. I had never spoken to him and had only seen him at work a few times. I found him to be extremely attractive. As we approached the pump at the same time, he turned to me, smiled, and said, "you ready for this long trip?". I responded by nodding my head and muttering "uh, huh". Internally, I was kicking myself! Erica, say something! This is your chance! However, the best I could do was "uh, huh".

Later in the week, on the last day of training, we are sitting in the "chow hall" (dining room) for lunch. I saw him in the line. I said something to the effect of "OMG, he is SO hot". My buddy Darren was sitting next to me and immediately springs into action. "Do you want me to be your wing-man?" I laughed and said sure. Darren approached my "crush" and they made a plan for us to meet up later that evening at a local pool hall. Traditionally the entire group gets together on the final evening after training is complete to celebrate and socialize.

That evening he and I talked, and the conversation seemed easy. We played pool, we danced, we had a few beers. When we arrived back at North Fort Hood, he walked me back to my dormitory and kissed me goodnight.

After leaving me that evening, he apparently returned to his dormitory and hazed some of the rookies. He made a few enemies that evening, and as a result, he rode back to Louisiana in my van. We talked much of the way home. He showed me pictures of his kids, and I showed him pictures of mine. I remember being confused about the ages of his children. He had 2 children with his ex-wife, and 2 children with an ex-girlfriend; however, they were staggered.

He admitted he had cheated on his ex-wife and impregnated another women. He and his wife "worked things out" and then had another child together. He claimed that when their marriage ended, he went back to the ex-girlfriend and they had another child. He seemed very sweet and sincere as he described the pain he caused his ex-wife and how sorry he was. He talked about what he had learned, how he was different.

I believed him. Red flag number one.

We exchanged phone numbers, and he asked if he could take me on a date. I was leaving as soon as we returned to fly to Oregon for a job interview. We made plans for the following weekend.

We texted throughout the weekend during my trip to Oregon. I sent him pictures of the coast. He said he wanted me to meet his mother. I remember being very excited at the possibility of a relationship with him.

When I returned to Louisiana, I told my friend and fellow psychologist Matt about everything that had transpired. His response was, "you know he has a girlfriend, right?" I was floored. I told Matt he hadn't mentioned a girlfriend, but that I hadn't specifically asked. I assumed because he agreed to meet up with me and asked me on a date, that he was single.

As soon as I was able, I called him and told him what Matt had said. I waited for his response. He said, "my bad. I should have told you. I am dating someone, but it is ending. I'm just waiting for her to get the rest of her stuff from my house. I can understand if you want to wait until that is all finished." I remember feeling very confused, but at the same time what he was saying seemed reasonable.

Red flag number two.

Yet I agreed to move forward with the date that weekend, thinking there was no harm in getting to know him. We went on several dates in May of 2010.

In June of 2010, I had to send my kids away to Michigan for the summer for the first time. I had never been away from them for more than a couple of weeks, but I couldn't afford childcare for the summer and my former in-laws offered to help. They were gone for 12 weeks. I was so lonely without them. I felt like a piece of my heart was missing. It was the worst summer of my life, at least at that time.

I did not know that it would get much worse.

While my children were gone, I turned to my new boyfriend Michael to fill some of the void of their absence. We spent much of our free time together. He'd bring me flowers and cards, and other small gifts. He said all the right things. He made me feel safe and comfortable. He spent the night at my house one night after a date and never left. He moved his toiletries and work clothes in.

Red flag number three.

I recall being very conflicted. I felt it was happening too quickly, and that I was losing my freedom and independence, but I didn't want to hurt his feelings and risk him moving on. The loneliness I felt without my children was deep and palpable. I wanted him around to fill that void. So, I went along with it.

By the end of the summer, my lease was ending on my rental house. He said, "you and the kids can come stay with me if you need to." Stupidly, I agreed. I didn't want my kids to come home from their summer to living in a strange man's home. So, I moved in briefly with my friend Erin and her son. My kids were close to Erin as well, and this was a mutually beneficial arrangement. We were both single mothers and could help each other with our children.

Disney Monday

Several weeks after moving in with my friend Erin, my kids came home. We took a trip to Florida to meet up with my best friend Katherine and her two kids. Katherine and I took our kids to Disney World for the first time. She and I and the kids had a great trip.

On Monday of that week, my boyfriend basically disappeared. I try calling and texting with no response. The same thing happened two days later. I remember feeling panic and overwhelm. My gut told me he was up to no good.

I said to Katherine, "I think he is cheating on me." She said I was crazy and that he clearly loved me. Why would he cheat on me? I can no longer remember his bullshit excuse as to why he didn't answer calls or texts. Something like, "Oh, I've been so tired recently and I fell asleep and didn't hear the phone."

What are we up to? Red flag number four?

When I returned to Louisiana and went back to work, a coworker called and told me my boyfriend had been at another woman's house twice while I was gone. I asked her when. She said Monday and Wednesday. She was best friends with the woman he had been with, so she was a credible source. I didn't want to believe her.

I immediately confronted him, and he had an excuse and explanation for everything. EVERYTHING. I believed him because I wanted to. He did such a great job of pretending to be someone he wasn't. Super caring. Super attentive. Very responsible and hardworking. Made me feel like the most important person in the entire world.

How could he do this to me? How could he cheat on me? He played to my weakness and vulnerability. I was a young single mom with a good job and a bright future. He saw a paycheck. I saw my life partner. Someone that would truly be my equal and share the burden of life with me. Someone that understood how hard it was to work in a prison. How hard it was to live in Central Louisiana all alone with no friends or family.

So, I believed him. I believed him and I said yes when he asked the kids and I to move in with him. Entries from my journal illustrate my dilemma and the internal struggle I was having to make sense of everything.

August 25th 2010

I don't know how to get past the fear, the doubt, the constant thoughts about Michael being at her house. All seemed feasible. I wasn't here. He was sad, lonely, bored. The right female came along at the right time. As he said, Cristy said he told her he had no intention of breaking up with you, that this was just going to be something on the side.

I feel sick writing this. I feel a tightness in my chest. This is completely feasible. I think I know him, then again maybe I don't. I'm so in love I could be totally blind.

I'm intentionally not pursuing the truth, whatever that may be. I'm not sure I can handle the truth. What if it happened? What if he went over there twice and had sex with that nasty whore? Who else has he been with? Who else calls? Who else emails?

Am I stupid? Stupid to trust and believe so fully in someone and rely so heavily on them that I opened myself up for the greatest pain I've ever felt? WTF? Am I stupid? Am I? Maybe so. Oh well, fool me once shame on you fool me twice shame on me.

I wish to move past the Shelly incident and move on with my life. I need to refocus on me. Take off the blinders. Open up the tunnel vision and move forward. Whether or not he did, it is in many ways irrelevant now because I've chosen to be with him. Katherine says maybe I should just believe him.

Maybe I should.

That would make all of this better. Just trust what he tells me. But something tells me not to. I've been praying about it. I'm not sure if my prayers are working or being heard though. I guess I should focus on praying for inner peace for trust and for God to guide Michael in the right direction so he does not stray in the future. I want to be able to trust him again. I had no doubts before. None whatsoever. Then this. Now I can't seem to rest or get some Peace of Mind.

I hate it that I'm here trying to get my head right by writing, and I'm worried about what he is doing and thinking. Dear Lord I want this to go away. I want my happy life back where I was going to live with him very soon and move forward. I want to refocus and get back on track with all aspects of my life. I just want positive things and positive people in my life.

I think moving in with Michael would be a positive thing in many ways as it will alleviate many fears and concerns etc. I'll get to see him every day and sleep next to him every night. I'm tired of living out of suitcases and boxes. I want order and organization back in my life. Maybe I just need to believe him. Maybe it never happened. Believe that Shelly is an evil psychopath and that her day of reckoning will come.

I know he loves me. I know it. You can see it in his face feel it in his touch. You can tell by the things he does. He is very good to me. Has never given any indication that he can't be trusted. I don't know why he would risk losing everything for some stupid woman. But he is a man. Men will cheat because they can.

If my partner wants to cheat on me to violate that trust and take advantage, I want to still wake up every morning knowing I'm a good person and I deserve to be treated like a Queen. I deserve to be with someone that recognizes the gift of me and is worthy of that gift. I pray that if he did mess up, that he realizes what he would be losing and that the cost is not worth it. That I am worth resisting any temptations that may arise. I believe he sees that. I believe he knows I'm worth any hard work he would have to do such as the hard work of resisting female companionship when it presents itself.

That fall I came home to the electric being cut off for lack of payment.

This is the first of many financial red flags, but overall red flag number five.

I called the electric company and paid the bill to get them turned back on, confused as to how he didn't pay the bill. I gave him plenty of money each month for my share of the rent and bills. Again, he gave me an explanation that I wanted desperately to believe, so I did. Money was something we seemed to agree on in terms of how to spend it and save it, however I quickly noticed his actions and his words often did not align.

September 26th 2010

I'm going to f-ing lose it right now. I'm in a pissy mood. Earlier I thought maybe some money was missing from our savings jar, but I didn't want to overreact. I counted $25. Later I go to put some clothes away, $19. $6 missing? Did it grow legs and walk away? Really? Really? I can't calm down. I need to calm down. I need to relax. Relax. Relax. Why is this happening? Get it together Erica. Get it together. Red flags. Pay attention to the red flags. I feel like my trust has been and is being violated. How hard is it to say "babe I'm low on cash going to borrow a few bucks from the jar." Then put a note in there detailing how much you took then pay it back. I'm so upset right now. I'm feeling better as I write but upset still. I want to go home. Pack my kids and go home.

On Christmas, he proposed during a trip to New Orleans. We had been dating about 8 months by this time. Part of me felt ecstatic! Part of me screamed "what are you thinking??"
I said yes.

For a while things seemed to go well. I started to relax a little and trust that my hesitations were old fears. In July of 2011 I came home from work one day while the kids were again gone for the summer. As I walked to the door, I saw an eviction notice stapled to the door frame. My fiancé was in Colorado at New Lieutenants Training.

My heart began to race. I felt sick. Everything started to spin. "How could this be? I give him money for the rent? How can we be getting evicted?" I went inside and called the property manager. They told me we are nearly $4000 behind in the rent. Our rent was less than $600 a month. I just didn't understand.

I called Michael, and he apologized. I can no longer remember what bullshit excuse he gave me, but he apologized profusely and promised to do better. I took over paying the rent just like I did with the electric bill. Groceries? I bought them. Phone bill? I paid it. Car insurance? I took that over as well.

I know. I feel like an idiot. I understand that now. But I bought the story he sold me. I wanted my perfect fairy tale ending and the narrative of having an irresponsible, womanizing, narcissistic, emotionally abusive husband did not fit in my fairy tale. Looking back on my writings during that time the emotional abuse is obvious now. It was not obvious to me then.

Summer 2011

I'm so frustrated right now. I feel like I'm trying very hard to be a good fiancé. I praise him, I tell him how much I love and respect him how much I appreciate him etc. I know I'm not perfect, but I sure am trying to be. But I feel like I can't do anything right. Every time I turn around, I've done something wrong. I've looked at an old card. I've talked too much. I can't raise my kids right, I tried to get him to move before he's ready.

Tonight, I've apparently left too many pictures on Facebook of myself with my ex-husband. I get it. That would upset me too. I don't mind deleting that crap, but I just want it all to stop. I don't like feeling scared that I've messed up and he's going to leave. I feel paranoid all the time because I don't want him to think I've cheated.

I haven't done the first f-ing thing wrong in this relationship. I don't talk to any male friends anymore. I don't even talk much at work for fear someone will try and start some drama.

I constantly feel anxious that he's hiding something he thinks or feels. He always is so paranoid and suspicious. He cheats when he thinks he's being cheated on. It's like he wants to catch me messing up so he always looks for it. Well, he can look all he wants. I haven't nor do I intend to ever mess up. My fear though is that he'll convince himself I am messing up and will start cheating.

I guess I'm not real confident lately that this is going to work. Will we make it down the aisle? I guess that remains to be seen. I love him more than anything, but I can't live my life with this constant feeling like I'm going to lose him at any second because he thinks I'm a tramp.

You know what? F you for being so judgmental and harsh. You aren't perfect. You have three baby Mamas and you've got another woman pregnant while married to your ex-wife. That is some straight BS right there. You go ahead and judge me. Go ahead and mess up. I know I'm alright. I'm doing all the right things. When it comes down to it and I have to answer to someone at the end of my life I'll be able to hold my head high knowing I did the right thing.

I'm really not sure what to do. Should I run while I can? Should I move home and focus on myself and the kids? Should I tough it out and hope it all gets better? I want to do what's right by everyone involved. I would never intentionally hurt him. I know leaving him would hurt, but so would being married and miserable.

I feel burnt out this week like I've given so much and received nothing. He's had a long week for some reason. He says it's from working morning watch on Sunday night. I just want to be happy, to be loved unconditionally. To be given a second chance to do it right. I'm trying so hard to take good care of him to be a good wife so he'll always be happy and always smile and never be that guy that complains at training that his wife is annoying or nags or doesn't have sex enough.

I just want to erase Disney Monday. God how awful. Erase it. Erase me reading things I didn't want to read, me knowing things I didn't want to know. Take me back to when I believed he thought I was perfect. Back to when I never questioned his honesty or integrity. I love him and want to be with him for the remainder of my life, but only if I can do so with a clean slate. I'm giving him the second chance he deserves. I want mine. I feel I deserve it. Deserve to be blissfully happy.

We can have that, but we have to let go of the past. Leave it where it is. I need to learn how to find happiness within myself and peace within, and not rely so much on him to dictate my happiness. I should be able to be happy no matter what. I am not 100% sure how to accomplish this but it needs to be done.

November 2011—Several days before our wedding I broke out in hives all over my face and chest. I went to the doctor, and he told me it was stress. Probably from planning the wedding. In hindsight, it was body saying "what the fuck are you doing???? Run. Don't walk. Run away from this man while you still can."

I couldn't run away. Invitations had been sent out. Money had been spent. Family had made travel arrangements to come. So, I pushed the thoughts away.

Our wedding was beautiful. I felt very happy and content. I had a great weekend with my close friends and family in New Orleans, followed by an amazing honeymoon. There were a few moments both at the wedding and on the honeymoon where I could see the regret on Michael's face, but I pushed it away as nerves.

I remember a conversation one day on the balcony of our cruise ship. We were discussing the success of marriage and how happy we were. He said that this time, (he was married previously) he wanted to do the right thing, and that he hoped he could. I was confused by this statement.

Anyway, flash forward to our honeymoon and the statement on the balcony. I thought to myself, "You hope you can do it? You hope you can stay faithful and do the right thing? Really?"

I remember being hit with a wave of panic, thinking about him having a baby with someone else while married to me. That was my worst nightmare. I felt so bad for his ex-wife. I couldn't imagine the pain she felt. Years later, I would. But then, I let it go.

December 2011—My Grandma Heinzman, one of my favorite people in the entire world, got very, very sick. I had less than 24 hours to drive from Louisiana to Ohio, praying that she would hold on long enough for me to get there to say goodbye. That day, my husband played the role of the perfect supportive spouse, stepdad, and son-in-law.

I arrived at the hospital at 4:30am. She was unconscious by then, but still alive. My grandpa and I were able to share a moment together before he resumed his place beside her, holding her hand.

I went over to her, smoothed her beautiful curly hair - hair that as a tiny girl I loved to comb and brush and put in pink foam curlers and pig tails. She'd sit in a tiny yellow rocking chair in the middle of their living room, allowing me to play beauty salon with her as my patron. I smoothed her hair, kissed her feverish forehead and told her how very much I loved her and thanked her for waiting for me. She passed away several hours later once my mom, my stepmom, my dad, grandpa, uncle, and myself were all surrounding her. She waited for me. I know she did.

My husband was a pallbearer. It meant a lot to me that my family would ask him to do that. Years later when he betrayed me and our relationship, I remember thinking back to Grandma's funeral and being disgusted that he carried her to her final resting place. He did not deserve the honor of carrying that sweet, silly, sometimes irrational and impatient, but always loving, woman. I hated him. But that's to come.

After my grandmother's funeral, we returned to Louisiana. In January 2012 I was offered a position as a Residential Drug Abuse Program Coordinator for a penitentiary in Beaumont, Texas. I was torn about what to do. I did not want to go to another USP but knew the position would be an excellent career builder.

While my husband was at work, I texted a coworker about the job. He was also a psychologist and had been an intern at the same location as me only a few years later. I had helped mentor him as he was considering a job at USP Pollock. When my husband got home and I mentioned I had been chatting with this coworker, he became enraged. He could not understand why I would talk about such a personal decision with anyone other than him. I felt terrible. I hadn't meant to upset him. I was just trying to get the perspective of another BOP psychologist.

Following this incident my coworker strangely stopped talking to me. If I texted, no response. If I saw him at work, he would turn and go the other direction. We had a staff retreat at a local historical site, and he did everything he could to avoid me. I sent him an email at work asking what was going on. I asked my husband about it and he denied any knowledge. He stated, "I haven't talked to that dude in a while."

I would later learn that my husband went to work, called that coworker down to the special housing unit (SHU), grabbed him by the throat, held him against the wall, and threatened, "if you ever fucking talk to my wife again, I'll kill you." I would later learn that this was not the only person that had such an encounter with my husband.

Climbing from Rock Bottom

It wasn't until years later I would learn about "gas lighting" and emotional abuse. Because my husband never put his hands on me, I had no idea I was in an abusive marriage. I thought the problem was me. There was a pervasive lack of self-worth, strong feelings of self-loathing, and the thought that I deserved to be treated poorly.

Your brain has both a "rational" side and an "emotional" side. Ideally where the two intersect is where we function most of the time, being able to both feel our feelings and analyze them from a rational point of view. My rational brain knew I deserved much better. My emotional brain told me I should be happy that someone "loved" me and that perhaps I was overreacting.

Gas-lighting is a form of emotional abuse in which a person uses manipulative tactics to gain power. The tactics are often subtle and leave the victim feeling as if they are "crazy" or in the wrong. These tactics were present from the very beginning of the relationship, but I did not recognize them.

I wish I knew more about emotional abuse at that time. I wish my friends and family would have called it to my attention. I wish I would have known my own worth and put a stop to the abuse from the very beginning. I've climbed from rock bottom by knowing my value and worth and by striving to educate my children, my clients, my community on the signs of emotional abuse and how to escape.

Footholds

Family: Losing my grandma was very tough. Spending time with my family helped with the grieving process. Sometimes family can be the source of our pain or abuse. If this is the case for you, it is okay to set boundaries around spending time with abusive or toxic people. Many times, our family can be our soft place to fall when we are struggling. Family can be both blood/biological, created, or chosen. For me, my family is my soft place to fall. They love me and they give great hugs. This was always something that comforted me in hard times.

Gratitude: One thing that helped me through the passing of my grandmother was gratitude and remembering all of the happy memories. I could have chosen to focus on the loss and sadness and stay stuck there, but rather I chose to remember all of the important lessons she taught me, how she made me feel, and the fun times we had together.

Finding and expressing gratitude during tough situations helps the brain to balance painful and positive memories in that moment. It might not always be easy to find something to be grateful for during hard times. Somethings we can be grateful for our breath or grateful for the ability to learn and grow from a hard situation even if it sucks.

Connection: Connecting with friends and family helped me stay centered and focused. Even though connecting with a friend to process my decision about the new job ended up resulting in a loss of that friend, his advice and thoughts were helpful. When you are feeling lost or disconnected reach out to someone! Make a connection with a friend or family member. You will feel less alone in your struggles.

Gut Instinct: In terms of the footholds that helped me in my relationship, a big one was my gut instinct. From the beginning, my gut instinct told me not to believe him. Looking back, this is one thing I would change. I would listen to my body telling me what was going on.

Listen to your gut. Trust your intuition. You are wise. Don't doubt yourself.

Speaking Up: I spoke up and voiced my concerns, fears, and anxieties. Looking back, I realize Michael used manipulation, gas-lighting, and other emotionally abusive tactics to dismiss my concerns. If I could go back, I wouldn't back down. I'd speak my truth and trust my instincts.

Speak your truth in order to care for yourself. No one else in the world can tell you that your feelings aren't valid. They are yours. Others may not agree with you and that is okay. In the words of Jen Sincero in *You are a Badass*, "Do not give one single crap what anyone else thinks of you."

Courage: I used courage to face the situation. However, I allowed fear to dictate my ultimate response. I stayed mainly out of fear of abandonment and being alone. You deserve to be happy, respected, and treated well. Do not stay out of fear. Do not believe the story you are telling yourself about how you are not lovable and you deserve to be in your situation. Be brave! Be courageous! You are SO worth it!

Chapter Four:
Beginning of the End

April 2012—My husband and I went to New Orleans for my birthday. I had a panic attack during our dinner because he mentioned that he wanted to go to Texas and see his kids that weekend after we got home. I had a strange sense that something was going on that I didn't know about. I couldn't put my finger on it, but something wasn't right. When we returned, I acted like a lunatic, crying hysterically while he packed his bags.

April 15th, 2012

Here I am home without him. I feel something today and I can't quite put my finger on it. He is in Texas visiting his kids. Whenever he leaves, I fall apart. Then I act like a crazy woman and get mad at him. I am afraid when he leaves, he won't come back. That he will somehow realize he is happier without me.

I am home sick. I miss my friends. I miss my family. I miss having a community. It has been three years since I felt like myself and even then, I wasn't truly happy. Not sure I ever have been. I felt peaceful and content when Michael and I first got together. It changed after Disney Monday. Seriously that was so traumatic! I still have panic attacks and of course every time he leaves, I behave like an idiot. How do I get my peace and comfort back? I pray for answers. I pray to be fulfilled. Maybe I'm missing a sign, a clue, a road map. I don't know what to do.

I can't always be mad at and frustrated with him, but all of my needs are not met. What happened? When I was on my own, I got to a point of comfort. A point where I relied on myself to make myself happy. I was so confident and self-assured. I don't know what happened. I'm tired of feeling like this. I want to love life and appreciate what I am blessed with. I'm tired of the ups and downs.

He missed the spring festival at my kid's school. He would take another such trip a few weeks later to watch an Easter musical his youngest son was in. He claimed to despise their mother, the side chick from his first marriage. Almost every inter-action I had witnessed either between them, or on the phone, was negative and dramatic. However, when he got home and discussed the musical he slipped up and mentioned that he was standing with her at the musical and their son saw them and waved.

I thought, "You were standing next to her? You two hate one another." Then his story changed and he said they weren't standing next to one another. Hmm. Red flag number....I don't know. I lost count. I let it go.

May 2012—On the 5th of May, my husband called me from work telling me SORT needed to transport an inmate to Forrest City, AR and that he would have to take the overnight trip. I said okay and be safe. He later called and asked if I could bring his wallet to the prison for him. The kids and I did.

A few hours later, after dinner, the phone rings. The caller ID says it was from the prison where we both worked. The caller said, "Erica you don't know me, and I don't want to say my name, but you should know your husband is cheating on you with one of his baby mamas. They are staying right down the road from you at the Motel 6." I hung up on her.

The room began to spin. I struggled not to vomit. I blacked out momentarily. I was sweating profusely and in a total panic. I didn't want the kids to see me like this, so I excused myself and went upstairs. I began blowing up his phone. He hung up on a me a few times, claiming he was losing service. I acted like a lunatic, de-manding he put one of the other guys on the phone.

I called the prison and asked the operations lieutenant what time the SORT trip would return but he said, "Dr. Adkins, there is no SORT trip tonight." I told him that my husband said he was taking an inmate to Forrest City. He said, "let me call you back."

A while later he called back and said, "Yeah there is a trip. I didn't see the memo. They'll be back in the morning." I felt relieved, but not completely. My husband came home the next morning and sold me a story. I let it go.

In June of 2012 while home for my brother's wedding I caught my husband eye-balling one of the bridesmaids. I confronted him. He made me think I was crazy, and I dropped it.

Several weeks later, I went to Massachusetts to see my best friend Katherine. He decides to go see his kids that weekend in Texas. I felt uneasy, but how could I tell him not to go see his kids? He was broke, so I gave him some money from the savings account for gas to get there and back.

While I was at Katherine's, I had another situation where I would call and he wouldn't answer. He texted saying he's putting the boys to bed, and he'd call me later. He does, but he's weird and quiet. I feel uneasy. I let it go.

July/August 2012 – My kids were gone for the summer. We had all of my husband's children over to Louisiana for a week. This took a tremendous amount of coordination. I planned a fun-filled week including a trip to New Orleans to the zoo, the aquarium, and the insect museum, along with site-seeing. The girls and I did some shopping (he had an older teenage daughter from a high school relationship).

On the last day, my husband drove the oldest to Houston to catch her flight back to California. I kept the youngest 4 and took them to Chuck E Cheese. He texted me and said the boys' mom is "tripping" and so he is shutting off his phone. I immediately get a stomachache, because I imagine that drama will ensue in Louisiana as well.

Sure enough, the manager comes to find me and asks if I am there with 4 kids. I said yes. He said, "your sister is on the phone." I said "I don't have a sister. Please take a message." He returns with a name and phone number. It was her. The ex. I tell the kids we have to go home.

As we are driving, the oldest son asked me, "Is it my mom? Did we have to leave because my mom is upset?" I said yes. He just looked down at his lap with tears in his eyes. I told him not to worry. Everything would be okay.

We got home and she began to call the house phone repeatedly. I wouldn't answer. Pretty soon the cops showed up to do a "welfare check" on the kids. They were, of course, fine. I tell the cop what was going on with the crazy ex.

He said I could press charges for the phone harassment. I declined. He went on his way. I finally answered the phone. I told her I didn't want any drama, and that the kids were fine. I let her talk to them. When they handed the phone back to me, she said, "I don't know what kind of bullshit you and Michael are trying to pull, but I'll see you back in court for more child support because I'm pregnant." I hung up the phone.

The now familiar panic began - room spinning, stomach threatening to spill its contents, sweating profusely, can't catch my breath, heart racing. I tried to call my husband. It went to voice mail. I called his sister. She and her best friend came over to provide support. He got home several hours later. He insisted that the ex is crazy, that he doesn't know whether or not she was pregnant but that if she was, the baby was not his because he hated her and hadn't been with her. I wanted to believe him but I didn't.

The next morning, I had to leave for United States Public Health Service (USPHS) Officer Basic Course. I packed my things and tried to sleep. The next morning, I boarded my flight for my two-week training feeling as if my entire world was crashing down around me. I tried to let it go.

August 6th 2012

Officer Basic Course finally! I'm here! Yippee! 18 months later. Well, it has been off to an interesting start. My stomach is churning already with what I need to write about.

Last week's visit with the kids was great until Friday night when Marie lost her mind. Part of me feels like I don't understand her antics, while the psychologist in me knows exactly why she does what she does.

There are so many reasons to believe that what she is saying is all fabricated. If he were going to cheat, why would he choose her? Why would he risk losing friends and family in addition to losing me? That would make no sense.

But that seed of doubt has been planted. He would lose so much though. I pay most of the bills I help with his kids. I love and support him. I know he loves me. Everyone that knows him can attest to that.

He seemed genuinely upset by all of this drama with Marie. It is still totally plausible that he didn't go anywhere but here in town, but that doesn't explain everything. I've seen pictures of his boys asleep when he has them. She mentioned meeting him in Houston all the time. Whatever. I know for sure that isn't true. She is crazy and evil and she doesn't want him to be happy because she is not happy.

I feel like I need to just forget all of this happened and move on, but I don't know that I can. I guess the alternative is to accept that he has been inappropriate and focus on moving past it. If I really wanted to dig around and find out the truth I could. I don't want to be that girl though. I want to just love and trust my husband.

In December of 2012, I found out that I had been selected for a job as a Special Management Unit psychologist at USP Florence, in Florence, CO. One week later, I found out I was pregnant. One might question why I decided to have a child with this man considering I was unsure if his ex was pregnant, but he adamantly denied having anything to do with her, and she stopped calling. I wanted so desperately for my fairy tale to work. I felt like my kids deserved a family and I wanted a baby.

February 2013—We went to Colorado Springs to find our new house. I made an offer and ended up under contract with my dream home. It was a perfect house in a perfect neighborhood with perfect schools and a good job in COLORADO! I felt like everything was going to be okay.

From Colorado we drove to California to see my husband's family. On the drive back, as we crossed through New Mexico, I had a panic attack. Out of nowhere I was convinced that the ex was pregnant and that here I was pregnant as well and I just bought a house, and my life was going to be ruined. He lost his patience with me, told me how crazy I was, and asked why wouldn't I just let it go. "She's not pregnant!" he insisted. I tried my best. I pretended to let it go.

At the end of February, the kids and I packed up and moved to Colorado. My husband found out on the day we were having the house packed, that he had been selected as a lieutenant at USP Florence as well and would be joining the kids and me in 12 weeks. I cried hysterically as I drove away from him that Friday morning, somehow knowing that my life would never be the same.

We moved into our new house in March of 2013. My husband came to Colorado for the week to help. We had an ultrasound on Thursday, March 21, 2013 and learned that the baby was a girl. We celebrated. We went shopping for tiny pink sleepers and little purple socks. We picked out a crib and changing table. I felt complete. I felt at ease. I felt excited about my baby girl.

He went back to Louisiana at the end of the week. I felt lost again. Empty. Alone. I hated my new job. It was awful, working with the most vile, violent, and disruptive inmates in the entire bureau of prisons. I felt like a sexual object every time I walk into the housing unit and heard the constant cat calls, inmates exposing themselves, masturbating in order to shock and upset me. It was awful. Just awful. So awful that now when I drive down 115 in Colorado, the route to the prison, I get sick to my stomach. I barely remember any of the specific stories that I used to swear I'd write a book about. My book was going to be called *You Can't Make This Shit Up*.

Easter Sunday, March 31, 2013 is the day that changed my life forever.

The ex had created a fake Facebook profile and informed me that she and my husband had a baby boy on March 21, 2013. She gave his name, his stats, and his photo. He was adorable. I felt a strange mixture of emotions. Rage. Sadness. Horror. Relief. Fear. Love. I was relieved that I finally knew the truth. Relieved that I wasn't the crazy one. Relieved that I had been right all along. I felt love for the little tiny boy. I knew he had nothing to do with this. He was an innocent victim as well. He didn't ask to be brought into this drama.

Years later when we had custody of him and his two older brothers, he called me "Mommy" from the first day we picked him up. He and my daughter were practically twins, only 5.5 months between the two of them.

I digress though, on that Easter Sunday, earlier in the day, I was driving to the grocery store with the kids. I remember having the thought out of nowhere, "If his ex was really pregnant, she would have had the baby by now." It was almost like God was preparing me for what I would see on my computer later that day.

April 12th 2013

I need to get started on this healing process. Yesterday hearing my husband say the words "I had an affair with my son's mother, and she got pregnant" nearly killed me. I am so hurt. I feel at times like the pain will never end. But I know it will at least get duller over time.

I just want to feel better.

Less depressed, less anxious, less worried that my marriage will end. I'm reading books, we went to marriage counseling, and I have a counseling appointment on Wednesday. I want to rebuild and redefine my marriage. I just want it to work so bad. I don't want to lose my husband. Right now, I have no choice but to trust what he says about loving me and wanting this to work. How do I get past this hurt?

I have weighed pros and cons of staying with him and getting a divorce. Honestly, I really haven't thought very seriously about divorce. I just want to do everything I can to save this. I just need to focus on healing myself and moving forward with my husband. I love him and I know we can make it through this. It's just a matter of if we will.

I didn't skip a beat. I went to work the next day as if it hadn't happened. I told a few coworkers and they surrounded me with love and support. He of course admitted finally to having sex with her, but swore the baby was not his. I did the math. Based on his date of birth, he would have been conceived the weekend I was in Massachusetts with Katherine. He swore he didn't have sex with her then. I had had enough of his lies at this point. Part of me wanted desperately to believe him, to believe that the baby wasn't his. But I knew. As soon as I saw his photo, I knew.

Thus began 6 months of hell.

He was still in Louisiana. I began to suspect he had a girlfriend there. He of course denied. We began this ridiculous dance of me trying desperately to keep my family together for the sake of my baby girl, him claiming he'd do anything to fix things, but in the meantime had another girlfriend on the side. My job was hell. I was losing weight rather than gaining. I had a scary run-in with an Associate Warden in which I feared he was going to assault me, several scary run-ins with inmates, a tooth that got infected and needed to be pulled, and a partridge in a pear tree.

Prior to learning about the baby boy, we had moved into our house, but we were renting it from the seller due to our mortgage not closing on time. This was incredibly stressful, and I felt like I could not handle one more thing.

Then Easter happened when I find out about his baby. The following morning called my real estate agent and mortgage broker and said "Don't you dare put his name on my house." They were able to revise all of the closing documents and I closed 5 days after learning that my husband had a love child. My house. In my name. That I bought all by myself. I was NOT going to let him ruin what I had going.

April 14th 2013

He left a little while ago. I feel super anxious right now because I don't know if I can trust him. He lies about little stuff. He bought all these new clothes yesterday and I bought him cologne and he took it all back with him. It just makes me anxious and makes me feel like there is someone in Alexandria he is seeing also.

God that would suck.

I have no proof though none at all except suspicions. I suppose those are natural given what we've been through lately.

Maybe I'm an idiot. Maybe I'm getting played big time. He says he's bonded with our baby though, different than with his other kids, so maybe she will be enough to get us through if we just keep working on things.

I need to let this anxiety go. I love him and want him in my life, but I'm not a failure if he chooses someone else. I will just focus on me getting well and living the life I want with or without him. I desperately want it to be with him though.

He will be here for good in 20 days I would really like it to be sooner, but it will all depend on if he is able to get some admin time or not. I'm done pushing it at this point. I would really like to focus on me and being less anxious and depressed and maybe I'm being more physically active. I can do this. I can relax.

Climbing from Rock Bottom

There aren't too many rock bottom situations that will compare to learning your husband has had a baby with another woman. It is a unique situation for sure. There are certainly situations that are far worse and far more painful, but the depths of betrayal were taken to a new level.

I learned that even the most unthinkable betrayal is something you can heal from and that even then, you can move forward. I carried so much shame about this particular incident. I felt very paranoid that everyone was looking at me, feeling sorry for me, and thinking what an idiot I was for staying with him. I kept it to myself for the most part. I did not tell my mom, my dad, or my brother. I only shared with a few close friends.

I immediately sensed that I was not going to be able to move through this trauma alone and reached out to my best friend. This happens to be the same friend that years later would say to me, "Erica, rock bottom is where bad bitches are built." Her wisdom and guidance kept me moving forward and her reassurance let me know that no matter what happened I would be okay. That is a powerful lesson. A powerful message. No matter what happens you will be okay. One way or another. It won't always be easy. It will hurt. But you will be okay.

Footholds

Choice: At all times I was able to make choices about how I wanted to respond. Even if it felt like my only choice was to breathe and put one foot in front of the other, those were choices. Having choices is empowering. No matter what we AL-WAYS have a choice about how we are going to respond to a situation. Take a look at your current situation. What choices do you have?

Zoom Out: After learning the truth, I was able to "zoom out" and see the bigger picture. It would have been easy to get lost in the moment and only focus on what was happening and how I was feeling in that instance. Instead, I chose to zoom out and put the situation in perspective. Did it suck? Yes. Would it kill me? No. Would I be able to recover? Yes.

During and after a trauma, we can get "tunnel vision" and focus only on certain aspects of a situation. Zoom out and see the bigger picture for perspective. For me, zooming out meant focusing on what I knew to be true despite the traumatic betrayal. I knew I was loved by friends and family. I knew I had a career and coworkers that would support me and allow me to financially support myself. I knew I had 2 beautiful children and another on the way and nothing could take that from me.

Writing: Writing in my journal helped me process many hurts and traumas. Writing has been empirically shown to assist with trauma processing. If you don't write or journal on a regular basis, pick up a pen and paper and get started! There is great power in writing and telling your story. Writing your story can allow you the freedom and ability to reread it and see what messages you might unintentionally be sending to yourself. It's your story to tell and you can choose the perspective from which you tell it.

For me I had the choice to have my story be about pain, misfortune and loss. While those elements were certainly present, my story was so much more. My story is about struggle, strength, courage and triumph. Your story hasn't ended. You are just at the start of a new chapter.

My 'Why': Early in my education I read the book *Man's Search for Meaning* by Viktor Frankl. Dr. Frankl was a psychiatrist held as a prisoner in a Nazi Concentration Camp during WWII. In his memoir he talks about how he responded to his circumstances in the prison camp. He spoke often of his "why" or his "reason" for how he responded and why mentally he kept going.

Returning back to my "why", my reason for moving forward, helped me to stay focused. My children are my "why". I always tried hard to make choices and decisions based on their needs and best interests. When I felt I couldn't go on any further, the thought of them kept me going. What is your "why"? Getting clear on your "why" can help provide clarity for you to see the next steps in your healing journey.

Chapter Five:
Here We Go Again

May 2013 – Michael was still living in Louisiana. The day he was supposed to leave there to move, he called me and said he's having a lot of pain in his leg and goes to Urgent Care. He then informed me he has a rapidly progressing cellulitis and had to go to the ER. He was admitted to the hospital, and needed surgery. I made arrangements for the kids and hopped on a flight to Louisiana.

When I walked into his hospital room, he was not pleased to see me. I felt very confused and hurt by his reaction, but played it off. He had Popeyes chicken next to his bed. I asked about it. He said one of the SORT guys brought it to him, and I believed him.

I tried to get comfortable in the hospital chair to sleep. After seeing this, Michael summoned a nurse and asked her for a pillow and blanket for his wife. The nurse stopped dead in her tracks, looked at me, turned her head as if she were confused, and then said, "okay," and returned with the requested items.

Her response would make sense to me weeks later.

Michael had surgery scheduled for that Monday morning. On Sunday I went to his hotel to take a shower. I noticed the framed picture I had given him of our wedding was not displayed. He had changed the picture on the iPad to one of his kids instead of us. There was a half-melted candle on the nightstand. I found several other strange things and knew a woman had been in there.

I asked him about it at the hospital, and big surprise, he denied it and said I was crazy. He had surgery Monday, and afterwards I went to the hotel, packed all of his belongings, and we began the drive to Colorado. I felt somewhat at peace. I felt like once he was back in the house with us, he would see that he wanted his family. He would work at it, and he would fight for us. But instead, he resented me. He told me I was making him miserable and that he just wanted to be able to do his own thing. I felt hurt, but I gave him space. I began to mentally prepare for a future with someone who didn't want me.

May 2013 – Toward the end of the month he insisted he had to return to Louisiana for a union arbitration. I didn't believe him, but he went. We had seen two different marriage therapists by that time. The first didn't work out because of his schedule. He didn't work late enough hours to accommodate us. The second was a nice man with evening availability. We went to one session prior to the "union arbitration" trip. Before my husband left for that trip, he placed small sticky notes all over the house with messages such as "I love you" and "I'll miss you." Well played.

June 2013- We had planned to spend the weekend in Chicago when we flew my children to spend the summer with their dad. He had forgotten about the trip and was very upset when I reminded him. I was confused. The trip was strained, and he didn't want to do anything with me. He didn't want to walk around, didn't want to sightsee, and didn't want me around. At the hotel the first night, I started crying while we were watching a movie. I knew it was over but was hoping I was wrong. He tried to comfort me, but I could tell he really didn't give a shit. He kept finding reasons to leave the hotel room. He needed to go buy a Sprite. He needed to go find something else.

That Sunday evening, we flew back home. I sat in middle seat, my head on his shoulder looking past him out the window. He reached over and put his hand on my leg. Tears began to stream down my face at this small gesture of kindness. The sunset was beautiful that evening. We were flying towards it. I remember thinking in that moment "fly faster! Don't let the sun go down! Don't let this day end. Don't let this moment end." I wanted to chase the sunset. To keep the future from happening, because I was uncertain what it would hold.

One week later he left me. He informed me via email at work that he had written me a letter. I got excited. I thought to myself "This is it! He is finally going to apologize and take accountability for his actions and tell me he wants to fight for us!" On the drive home, I asked him if I could read it. He said he'd give it to me after dinner. Dinner came and went. I asked again. He said he'd give it to me tomorrow.

At this point I was sure it wasn't good. I didn't sleep that night. I woke up the next morning and snuck downstairs. I rummaged through his work bag and found the letter. In the letter he told me he was leaving me, that he didn't want much, just some towels and some dishes and maybe one of the couches. I wish I could remember what else it said. I put the letter back and tried to pretend everything was normal.

After I read the letter, I sat on the couch watching television waiting for him to wake up. He finally came downstairs, made his coffee and sat on the other end of the couch. I said, "I'm guessing since you haven't given me the letter yet, it isn't good news." He said, "No, it isn't. Would you like me to get it for you?" I said, "Just tell me what's in it." I no longer remember what he said. I do know he mentioned he had secured his own apartment and already had the keys to it. He got up from the couch and began packing his things.

We were supposed to go have a 3-D ultrasound of our daughter that day to see her little face. He asked if he could still come to the appointment. I said, "Sure."

After he left with his first load of belongings, I sat in the bathroom and called my mom. "My husband just left me," I said. We cried together. Then I told myself to get my ass up and handle my business. I couldn't afford to just roll over and do nothing, so I changed my clothes and jumped in the car. I went straight to the bank to make changes to my account so that he could not take all of our money.

It's funny how God places people in your life at just the right moments. I sat down at the bankers' desk. Her name was Merced. She asked how she could help. "My husband left me this morning. I need to be sure he can't take all the money." Merced jumped into action. I was clearly pregnant, but stoic and poised. If I was freaking out inside, I didn't let it show. I held my head high and marched forward.

Merced closed our account and opened one in my name alone. She helped me order new checks and plan for a few other things.

After that I went to the AT&T store and separated our cell phone accounts. I can't remember the gentleman's name that helped me, but he was amazing. When he approached me and asked what I needed, I told him, "My husband just left me this morning. I need my own cell phone account." He did not flinch, did not skip a beat, just jumped right in to take care of me. He helped me make the changes. He talked to me while he was working, expressing his empathy for my situation. I told him not to worry about me. I was a tough broad. He said he could tell.

That afternoon I went to the ultrasound place. My husband was there as well. He sat on a little couch in the ultrasound room, while I lay on the table. The ultrasound technician played some beautiful music while scanning my belly. She was creating a video of the experience. The tears rolled down my face the entire time. Tears of sadness. Tears of sorrow. Tears of grief.

I knew she was coming into the world in the middle of a super fucked up situation. I felt terrible for her. I felt afraid for myself. How would I single parent 3 kids? One an infant? After it was over, I hopped in my car and went to the mall. I needed maternity clothes. At the maternity store, the clerk was super helpful. I don't know why, but I told her, "my husband just left me. I feel a little overwhelmed. Can you help me pick out some stuff? I need bras and I'd like some summer dresses." She was amazing. Super helpful. Super supportive. Super loving.

After my shopping trip I got some ice cream and went home. The emptiness in the house made me nauseous. I put my ice cream in the freezer. Untouched. My midwife had me come to her house. She had ordered me a personal-sized pizza from Pizza Hut to try to get me to eat. My phone buzzed non-stop with text messages from friends and loved ones, making sure I was okay.

After a while, I went home. I dreaded the silence that I knew awaited me. I tried to sleep without success. Sunday, I got up and went to church. I don't remember what I did after that. Monday morning, I got up and went to work. I was taking over the on-call duty for the week. My first on-call at FCC Florence was the week my husband left me. Outstanding. That Monday morning, I was supposed to attend a briefing at the facility where my husband was working. I knew I'd see him and was not ready for that. I made the decision to tell my boss what had happened. He was super supportive.

On Tuesday I was sitting in my office with my coworker. We were essentially trapped in there as the orderly was waxing the floors in the hallway. My phone rang. "Psychology, Dr. Adkins," I said.

"Hi Dr. Adkins. This is Officer O'Shannon from FCC Pollock. I need to talk to you about something, but it's not work related."

I asked him what the hell he was talking about. "You call me at work to tell me you need to talk to me about something non work related? I don't even know you."

He said "I know you and your husband are separated. I need you to help me get my wife back." He goes on to tell me that his wife, also an officer at FCC Pollock, has been seeing my husband since February. He stated she was very confused and wanted to leave him for my husband.

My heart was pounding and the room began to spin. It all made sense now. The second I left Louisiana, he, unable to be alone, found a girlfriend. She had been staying with him at the hotel. He had been buying her things with our money. Taking her out for drinks and dinners. Every single time I had a gut feeling that he was up to no good, he was.

I took down the officer's phone number and agreed to call him after work. My coworker immediately tells me he is so sorry he overheard the conversation, and that we needed to tell our boss. My husband was this woman's supervisor, so the relationship violated BOP policy. I said okay.

Later that afternoon our boss came into my office. I told him everything. He told me I needed to write a memo to the Warden or find myself facing "Failure to Report" charges. I asked him to please give me the evening to process. He agreed. I had until close of business the following day to get a memo to him.

That evening I printed 3 months of phone bills. Her number was on there over 9,000 times between calls and text messages. I highlighted every single one. I didn't want to talk to her husband, so we texted back and forth all evening. I screen-shotted every single one and sent them to my work email. I consulted several friends and colleagues on the situation in terms of the reporting process. I did not derive pleasure in reporting him. It was humiliating. I had to go in front of my Warden and hand him a stack of paper with a memo on top detailing the events of the past few days. He appeared to be supportive. Told me to reach out if I needed anything.

Two days later I drove to Denver to pick up my best friend Katherine. She dropped everything and hopped on a flight to come out and help me pack the rest of his shit and get it out of my house. She also spent hours weeding the back yard as it was like a jungle. She cooked me meals. She rode with me to work on the weekend when I had to go see inmates on suicide watch. We watched movies. We laughed. She made me feel less alone. She promised we'd get through it. She accompanied me to my follow-up ultrasound. I drove her back to the airport then went to meet my friend Francis at a hotel in Denver.

Francis was there for the week for a training, and invited me to stay. I took a few sick days from work. She was amazing. She made sure I ate, rested, and helped me talk through some of the emotions. The hotel we were staying in had Sleep Number beds. While watching television one night, Francis was frantically pushing the buttons on her remote saying "I have no idea why this isn't working! Nothing is happening!" Meanwhile, my mattress deflated to the point in which I was sunk completely into the bed. We both realized at the same time that somehow the remotes had been switched. We both belly-laughed for a good five minutes. Every time I thought of that story in the months and years to come, I truly appreciated that laugh.

June 26, 2013

This is my first time writing since he left. I can't believe this is my life now. All alone. No husband. No dad for the baby. I'm going to be all alone. He has so many problems and issues and he cannot change. I need to let go and move on. Not sure how I'm going to be able to do that. I miss him, but at the same time I feel liberated. I'm not sure how to reconcile the two. He has been very angry with me for the past week. It was easier then. I didn't expect texts or communication. Then yesterday he starts being nice and it sucked me back in. I'm looking forward to going home and getting away for a bit.

I wasn't allowed to go back to work after that. The doctor said I could not work in the housing units around inmates. The BOP decided I was too much of a risk, so they wouldn't let me on the prison grounds. Great.

My friends Arric and Linda invited me to stay with them for a few days. They have a log cabin in the mountains. I arrived on a Friday night, and they had pizza for me. All weekend they took care of me. Arric cooked me breakfast, lunch and dinner. They made me comfortable. They surrounded me with love. We had many great conversations about how I was a "catch" and I deserved so much better.

Linda said at one point "Erica, in a relationship we all have to ask ourselves what we can bring to the table. Girl when you roll up to the table you bring the whole damn buffet!" This lifted my spirits, and stuck with me moving forward as I tried my best to remember I was worthy of so much more than what my husband was doing to me. During this conversation Arric said to me, "No judgment Erica. If you decide to get back together, no judgment. You are having a child together." I remember telling him that wasn't an option and that even if I wanted to, my husband didn't want me. In many ways Arric gave me permission to make the decisions that were best for me, and vowed friendship no matter what.

I decided to go to Ohio for a few weeks to pass the time. My family threw a baby shower. I spent time with my Grandpa touring rural Ohio where he and my grandma grew up. I was surrounded by so much love. While with my grandpa, I received a text from my husband telling me he missed me. I responded, and was kind. Then, he faded away again.

July 12th 2013

Made it to Ohio. My grandpa and mom picked me up. I feel bad because I didn't really want to talk or know what to say.

The weight of my pain is palpable, crushing, at times all consuming. I miss him.

He's being nice to me and that makes it hard for me to remember what all he has done.

The husband I know and love wouldn't have had so many affairs and wouldn't lie to me. He wouldn't risk his family and livelihood to have a relationship with an officer. I have to remind myself of all these things as the pain is so awful. I miss him so much.

I never imagined any of this to be possible. I thought we'd be together forever and would raise our daughter together as a family. Now I'm going to be alone.

I must remind myself of my strengths and also of the liberation I've felt in the past few weeks. I have been able to be more relaxed, less stressed. But I find myself still fretting about things such as what will he think when he sees my new stuff. Will he think I have someone else?

I still worry he'll think I'm in a relationship. I still want to explain and defend myself in relation to his recent accusations. That isn't fair because I did nothing wrong. It still makes me ill to think about being with another man.

Even now I only want him. I hope one day that will change. I hope I can open myself to a healthy relationship one day. But I'm not going to be ready for some time. My focus is on my children and being whole and happy alone not with a man. I don't know how I will ever trust again. It is going to take some time.

My mom sold her house and packed up everything she owned in order to move to Colorado with me to help with the kids. My aunt and uncle drove the moving truck while we drove my mom's car. My husband called while they were there. He had a flat tire and was at Walmart getting it repaired. His card was declined. Could I lend him $45 to get his tire? Sure.

I drove to Walmart and paid for the tire. He asked if he could come by and get more of his stuff. I said okay. He came over and I invited him to stay for dinner. I had made lasagna. He did. My uncle helped him load some of his furniture into my mom's empty moving van and he drove to my husband's new apartment and helped him unload it.

It would be another month before I'd hear from him again.

One day I drove to pick up the kids from school due to the rain. As we were getting back in the car my phone buzzed indicating a text message. It said, "I miss you. I miss us."

I rolled my eyes and heaved a sigh. "How do you expect me to respond to this?"

"I don't know. I was hoping maybe you feel the same way" he said.

I'm 9 months pregnant at this point, scared of going into labor by myself, feeling very confused about raising the baby on my own, and wondering why I wasn't good enough to be his "only". Why did he constantly have to cheat on me? We texted a bit back and forth. The next morning his car got repossessed for non-payment. Naturally he asked me for help. I told my mom. She cautioned me that if I kept bailing him out, he was always going to do this. I was worried he was suicidal, and I needed him to be with me when I had the baby, so I paid to get his car out of impound.

July 15th 2013

I am awake at 6:00 AM. I hardly slept last night thanks to him. I need to be done with him. I need to find the strength to tell him it's over and to move on. Yesterday didn't happen. He didn't contact me and say he missed me.

Just pretend it didn't happen.

Focus on everything you've already started to focus on, your kids, moving forward, reclaiming yourself. If you allow him back in, you will give all of that up.

Think of all the lies over the years, the suspicions, the checking of your phone, voicemail, email, Facebook. Think of the controlling patterns of behavior. Think of the anxiety.

The level has decreased since he left. You are calmer and happier. He can never be the man you deserve and the man you need him to be.
Cut your losses and move on.

Nothing wrong with being civil and nice to him. Nothing wrong with being friends.

Steroid use was admitted. That is another lie. More deceit. He's not honest with you about much of anything. He thinks only of himself. You are doing fine on your own.

You don't need him.

At 35 weeks pregnant I learned the baby was breech. This meant I could not have a home birth as planned. I was devastated. I did not want a hospital birth and did not want a cesarean. I began to try EVERYTHING to get her to turn. I tried acupuncture, moxibustion, chiropractic care, laying upside down on an ironing board, etc. Nothing worked. I scheduled an appointment with my OBGYN at Fort Carson to try to flip her. The appointment was schedule for several weeks later.

August 13th 2013

Tomorrow we have a procedure to try and turn my baby girl. I've been praying for her to turn on her own. Now my prayer focuses on the doctors and nurses being able to turn her tomorrow.

I've realized in the past four to five months that I'm not in control of anything and I need to surrender. This has not been as scary of a process as I would have thought.

Now that my kids are home, I feel a renewed sense of purpose and hope for the future. I enjoy how things have been going. They're both so sweet and helpful. I've done a good job as a mother. I have been down on myself about being a bad parent but really that is far from true.

I love and cherish them and do my best to give them all of the experiences they want. I am a good mom. I feel like I am a better mom without him around. When he is here, I am focused on him and his mood and happiness and he is usually grouchy. So now that he's gone, I can relax and focus on my kids. I have no desire right now to be pursuing anyone or anything else.

Yesterday he texted that he missed me. We texted for a while and he mentioned wanting to work on us. I didn't know how to respond to that. I don't really think he's ready to change his behavior or his lifestyle. I guess we'll see. But even if he is ready to change that doesn't mean I have to take him back. He betrayed me, my trust, my children, my family and my friends.

All people who loved him unconditionally like me.

He walked out on me at seven months pregnant and has left me alone to be pregnant and running a household. I'm not sure I can move past that.

Forgiveness is the easy part.

Moving past the pain hurt and betrayal will be the hard part.

Right now, I don't have to deal with his finances, his baby mamas, his mood swings, his self-centered narcissism, his emotional abuse, his checking behaviors, his delusions, his infidelities.

All I have to deal with is me, my finances, my children. That's all. So much liberation! I feel so free. I also don't feel as sucked into him and his drama. I don't have to respond immediately to a text. He doesn't respond to mine.

He doesn't like it, but I owe him nothing. In fact, he gets far more from me than he deserves still. We shall see what today, tomorrow, and the next few weeks brings. We will see how serious he is about being involved with the baby when she arrives.

I'm going to allow him as much contact as he desires but I'm going to do my damnedest to protect my vulnerable heart.

On August 15 he accompanied me to the appointment at Fort Carson for the doctor to try to flip the baby. It worked. We headed home. He went back to his apartment.

August 18th 2013

My baby turned! Yahoo! Now we wait for her to decide when she's going to make her arrival. I worry about my husband. He is at rock bottom. He says he's ready to come home. I told him he had to work on himself. He says he's going to. I guess we'll see. As I told Katherine earlier, I am in a good place, a different place. I know I'm OK without him. I don't feel the desperation and anxiety. I do feel some hope and feel like he can change if he really wants to. I'm just guarding my heart right now. I love him and it's been great having him around the past five days. I hope it lasts. I really do.

Several false labors brought him to the house. Finally, on August 31, 2013, the day before my due date, he spent the night at the house. He decided to stay until the baby arrived.

On Wednesday, September 4, 2013, he accompanied me to my midwife appointment that morning. She told me I'm dilated 4 cm and effaced. Shouldn't be long. I labored throughout the day, and at 8:42 pm my baby girl was born at home in the bathtub. Her dad was there to catch her and place her on my chest. Her whole family was crowded into my bathroom to greet her in her first minutes of life.

He didn't leave after that. He stayed every night and helped me as we struggled with breast feeding, as the baby struggled with severe reflux and laryngomalacia. He went to every doctor's appointment.

About 3 weeks after she was born, he said to me, "If It's cool with you, I've rented a Uhaul and I'm going move my stuff back home."

It wasn't cool with me. I was exhausted. I was hormonal. I was tired. I wanted to say, "Hell no. I'm not ready for you to move back. You left me."

But I watched as my son had his head on my husband's shoulder while we were at my daughter's soccer game. How could I deny my children? How could I take away my baby girl's Dad? I felt defeated. I felt like I couldn't say no. He had already decided what he was doing. I told myself the baby deserved this. She deserved a chance. I told myself that he could stay until he screwed up again, which I was certain he would do. I didn't want my baby girl's story to be, "My Dad left my mom. He tried to come back and make amends and be with me, but my mom wouldn't let him". I wanted her story to be, "my dad loved me enough to come back. My mom loved me enough to allow him." So I did.

Climbing from Rock Bottom

I feel proud of the decisions I made during this chapter of my life. As difficult as it was to let him get close to me again, I knew that it would be important for my daughter's story as she grew up. Even if things didn't work out between us, I allowed him the opportunity to try to fix things. If I had it to do all over again, I am not sure I would have made some of the same decisions prior to becoming pregnant with my daughter. I probably would have ended things at the first red flag. However, I would walk through every single painful moment all over again if it meant having my daughter at the end of it all. She is worth every second of pain and suffering. I had choices in how to respond. I knew there would be consequences no matter what. At the end of the day, I had to make the decisions that would allow me to sleep at night.

Footholds

Perseverance: I made the conscious decision to fight, to move forward and take charge of my life and to minimize any damage he could do to me. Whatever is going on in your life, you can do this! You are a fighter and you can take charge of your situation! Putting one foot in front of the other is the definition of perseverance! You are moving forward toward resolution with each step you take.

Laughter: Laughter is a great protective factor. My friends tried their best to help me laugh. Focus on any area of your life where you can laugh. Watch a funny movie. Go to a comedy club with friends. Recall funny stories from your past. Laugh!

Acceptance: I recall having the thought, "This is it. This is your reality now. You have to accept it," and so I did. Acceptance allowed me to then move into problem-solving mode. What needed to be changed or accomplished in order to protect myself and my kids? Radical acceptance is the act of totally accepting the situation at hand without judgment. Accept the situation fully and then focus on any actions or changes you can take to move forward.

Empowerment: I felt like I was in control of my emotions and reactions. This was very empowering. Focus on the areas where you feel strong and empowered and use them to help bolster you during hard times. You are so much more than what has happened to you and you WILL rise above.

Determination: I was determined to be okay. Not being okay was not an option. Use your determination and your drive to propel you in the direction you want to go.

Control: I focused on what I could control. I could not control my husband or his actions. I could control my immediate environment and my reactions. I did not base my actions on him. Focus on what you can control. Don't dwell on the things you cannot.

Chapter Six:
Released From Prison

Five and a half weeks into maternity leave I received an upsetting call. I was supposed to be home until the first week of December. I had saved 6 weeks of annual leave in order to extend after my 6 weeks of paid maternity leave was over. I received a call on a Wednesday from my new boss. She had started at FCC Florence after I had gone on leave.

She said, "Hi, this is the new Chief Psychologist at Florence. I know you are on maternity leave, but I'm going to need you to come back to work on Monday when your leave is up."

I informed her that I wouldn't be back until December and that it had already been approved.

She said "I'm the Chief Psychologist. I didn't approve it. I can cancel any leave that was previously approved. I'll see you Monday."

I begged her to please let me stay home. I explained that I was breastfeeding and that the baby had some medical complications. Her response was "get a breast pump." I was infuriated. I had 2 days until I had to return to work.

As I hung up the phone with her, a fire ignited inside of me. Within 24 hours, I had signed the lease on a small office, jumped on LegalZoom and set up an LLC, secured a phone number, created a website, and began marketing myself for private practice. I had to stay with the BOP until April 2014 due to contractual obligations, so I planned to start part-time with private practice and transition out of the BOP. That's exactly what I did.

My final day at USP Florence was Friday June 13, 2014. I locked my keys in my car twice that day at the prison. The first time the guys from the lock shop helped me out. The second time was at the end of the day and they were gone. I had to wait for AAA to come. I thought, "Why? God, are you torturing me by keeping me at this miserable place longer than I need to be?" Finally, I was free. I felt like it was my release date from prison, and I was going home.

Shortly after my release from prison, my husband was demoted due to the inappropriate relationship he had with the female officer. He lasted about a month before he quit. The shame and humiliation of being an officer again after being a lieutenant was too much for him. We decided he'd stay at home with the baby while I worked. My mom moved back to Ohio. Life continued seemingly normal for a while. Frankly, I was shocked he had made it this far without screwing up again. I had anticipated he would have made it 2 months, tops, before he was up to no good.

July 6, 2014

So many things on my mind lately and wanting to talk to him, yet when we are together, I can't seem to find my words. As we prepare for yet another transition, I'm left feeling very alone and very scared. So far it seems all of the pressure to provide both finances and health insurance is falling on me.

The stress can be overwhelming at times. What if I can't do it? What if I fail?

Then there is the fear of the unknown. What if he cheats again? What if he's cheating now? Am I being used? Have I been being used all along? What purpose have I served? The lies and the cheating had been so pervasive throughout our entire relationship.

I might look stupid but I'm not. Someone doesn't go from all that lying and sneaking around to suddenly being a saint. Things are so much better since we started seeing a therapist in December.

Many days I allow myself to feel. To feel safe. To feel happy. To feel secure.

But lately I find myself questioning everything. I will never have the life I set out to have: one husband, one united family, a lifetime of love and trust. I married the wrong person for that the first time. That was my fault. With my husband now, I was so confident he loved and cherished me the way I had always dreamed someone would. I thought it would last forever. That all shattered mere months after the wedding.

I asked myself daily what does she have that I don't? What draws him back to her time and time again and am I ever going to be enough to keep him happy and keep him away from her? Am I enough to keep him away from any female? I don't want this to be my life. I don't want to have to worry about whether I will be enough. I am good enough. I'm beyond good enough.

During Christmas of 2014, we took a road trip to Ohio. We stayed with my brother and his family. After that, we drove to Louisiana. My friend Lyn was hosting an empowerment seminar and had asked my husband and I to be guest speakers and to talk about our journey. I was excited to speak. I had spoken at several other seminars that she hosted, and always enjoyed the experience. However, this time I had a sick feeling in my stomach. What if I get up there and talk about our story of forgiveness and redemption and then he screws up again and I look like even more of an idiot than I already do? But I agreed.

We both spoke at the seminar. When my husband spoke, he was emotional and finally said some of the things I had been needing to hear for a long time. He took accountability for his actions and talked about how he knew how much I had been hurt. I felt like perhaps I could have that happy ending after all. Perhaps we'd be a success story. Perhaps my daughter would get to have a family.

Last Saturday was powerful. I enjoyed telling my story. Afterward I felt empowered and it was a healing experience for me. Writing was very healing as well. It was cathartic. It helped me process through some of it and then reading it over and over prior to the seminar very healing. Lyn is right I need to toughen up and not allow Michael or anxiety about him to dictate my happiness. While he was gone, I felt at peace because my happiness was my responsibility.

When he came home, I was back to worrying about him, what did he want? What was he thinking? Was he happy? Was he lying cheating etc?

I realize how much of a prisoner I felt like. It's not his fault. It's mine for allowing it but placing fault isn't helpful. Realizing what's going on is the important part. The realization allows me to focus on what needs to happen. I would like to focus on being happy and content with myself.

The hopefulness was short lived. On February 11, 2015, just 6 weeks after the seminar, I get a text from my brother telling me he needed to talk to me. I adore my brother and would give my life for him, but we rarely speak or text, so when I saw this, I knew it had to be big. I called him immediately. He said, "I don't know how to tell you this, but your husband stole Jamie's (my sister-in-law) credit card and ordered stuff on Amazon."

He went on to explain how they found out, what was ordered, and that Jamie was filing a police report. The now familiar feeling of the room spinning, heart racing, face hot, chest hurting, and sheer panic and terror set it. He goes on to tell me that he had also tried to take out loans in my mom's name several months prior. My stepmom also had her credit card compromised after a visit to our home that previous September. I couldn't breathe. It was one thing to hurt me, but to hurt my entire family was more than I could bear. I come from an amazing family. We are hardworking, kind, generous, loving, giving people. No one in my family has ever intentionally hurt anyone. They don't lie. They don't steal. He violated my family.

At Christmas when we stayed at my brother's home, I left my husband alone at the house for 2 hours while I had breakfast with one of my best friends. During that time, he went through their house and found my sister-in-law's credit card. Months prior he went through my mom's documents in her room and got her social security number and tried opening loans in her name. He had gone through my stepmom's purse while she was at our house in September. I felt sick. I apologized profusely to my brother. He said it was okay, and that they weren't mad at me. They knew it wasn't my fault and that I'd never betray them. I offered to pay for any damages they suffered. He said no need as the bank credited their money back. All they lost was their sense of safety and security in their own home. We couldn't put a price tag on that.

I canceled my clients for the remainder of the day and headed home to confront him. He of course denied everything. Said I was crazy and that it wasn't him. I didn't listen. I told him he had two choices, he could own up to what he had done and tell me what the fuck was going on, or he could get his shit and get out, now.

He admitted to taking Jamie's card, but swore he didn't try to take loans in my mom's name. We went round for about an hour until he finally confessed to that as well. It would take a while for him to confess to my stepmom's card, but we eventually got there. I told him I knew he was on steroids again, and that clearly, he had a problem. He was stealing in order to buy his drugs. He admitted he had been on steroids for 15+ years. I only learned of his drug abuse while he was in the hospital. The infection in his leg came from an abscess deep in his thigh from a dirty needle. I had no idea he had been using our entire relationship and for many years prior.

The psychologist in me knew he needed some help. My values and my ethics guided my next steps. I told him he needed inpatient treatment and that was the only way the marriage would last. He had to find a place and do the legwork himself. He did. My mom came out and stayed with me for a month while he went to rehab. I was so embarrassed, ashamed, humiliated, angry, sad, depressed, etc. I felt like an idiot. I wanted him to leave. I wanted to leave him. I wanted out. But I felt trapped. He was my baby's Dad. He had no job. He was my husband. I had said, "I do. In sickness and in health. In good times and in bad." I felt obligated, so I stayed.

The entire month he was gone I felt free. I was able to live my life without answering to him. I was able to have conversations with friends without fear he would think I was cheating on him or lying to him. I would go visit on the weekends. Visits were often superficial and strained. Several times I tried to go and engage in family therapy. I felt very angry and frustrated that no one seemed to want to address the giant elephant in the room. This man had stolen from my entire family! I repeatedly asked when we were going to address that.

The therapist working with him commented that my anger was intense and that she didn't understand it. Truth be told, I have no idea how I did not snap in that moment and choke slam this woman. I understood she needed to develop a therapeutic alliance with him and be his advocate at times, but I also understood that he was there to be challenged and confronted about his substance abuse and behaviors associated with that. For this woman to not only dismiss my anger, but to insinuate that it was inappropriate was further infuriating. Clearly, he had sold them a sob story about his life and his situation, and they bought it just like I had. Seriously? Is he ever going to be held accountable for his actions?

The day came for me to go pick him up. I felt sick to my stomach. I was nervous. I was still angry. I was not ready to have him home. A different therapist asked me if I was excited to have him home. I couldn't even answer her. She patted my shoulder and said, "It's hard." We went home that day and he tried to resume our normal life. I wasn't interested.

I wanted to discuss hard things. I wanted to know the truth. I wanted to hear him say he was sorry and mean it. Our mutual friends came to our house that day to help him celebrate being home. The tension was so strong coming from me that they ended up leaving early. I felt bad because they were a huge support to me while he was away, but I was tired of dancing around his feelings and tired of putting on a happy face for everyone while my life was falling apart.

Climbing from Rock Bottom

I thought finding out he had a baby with another one was as bad as it could get. Boy was I wrong. It was one thing for him to hurt me repeatedly. I had made the choice to stay with him. But in my making the choice to stay with him, it opened the door for him to take advantage of my entire family. The shame and guilt I felt when my brother called me was something I had never felt before. It felt like it was my fault. If I hadn't stayed with him, he wouldn't have had the opportunity to violate the kindness and trust of my entire family. It was painful.

I feel so fortunate that my family is understanding and forgiving. They did not blame me. They did not say, "I told you so". They continued to stand by me. His betrayal made it difficult. Family is one of my core values. His betrayal put me in a position where I had to choose between my family-of-origin and my family with him and the kids. It was not an easy decision. I wanted out. I wanted to leave. I felt trapped.

Addiction is something that affects millions of families. The pain caused when the addicted person violates the trust of beloved family members is unlike any other. Like other traumas, having a family member struggling with addiction often carries a great deal of shame. It can be hard to talk about, so many families suffer in silence.

I wish I would have taken more advantage of programs designed for family members of addicts, such as Al-Anon and Nar-Anon. I suffered alone when there were plenty of resources I could have reached out to. If a family member or loved one is struggling with addiction you are not to blame. There are resources out there that can help you learn about your own behavior and ways you may be contributing to the cycle of use and abuse. You can choose to stop the cycle and set boundaries for yourself that protect both you and the loved struggling with addiction.

Footholds

Storytelling: Telling my story was very powerful. Standing on that stage looking out at an audience of women suffering from various traumas, I gave my pain a voice. I was validated for the hard things I've been through. After the seminar many women came to thank me and tell me of their own stories of trauma and addiction. I can only hope that telling my story empowered others to shed the shame and blame in order to tell their own.

Tell your story to someone that has earned the right to hear it. Be bold and brave and know that you are so much more than what has happened to you.

Free Will: No one decides my fate for me. This realization was very powerful and empowering. Take back control of your own destiny! Much like Viktor Frankl in *Man's Search for Meaning*, his physical body was controlled by the guards at the prison camp, but no one could control his mind. No one could take from him his choices on how to deal with the situation. No one could take away his "why."

You may not have had control over the things in your life that have happened to you or that you have experienced, but you can take control of the narrative moving forward and write your own ending.

Exposure: In preparing my speech for the seminar I wrote my story word for word. This was the first time I had done so. Writing, the reading, the speaking my story was basically "exposure" therapy, a therapy that helps decrease anxiety by allowing yourself to acclimate to the situation. Exposure therapy is an effective treatment for trauma. If you are not already working with a trained professional, consider finding one to help you in your healing journey.

I can't stress enough the importance of having a trained professional help you on your healing journey. There are many different forms of therapy to help heal from trauma. A licensed professional can collaboratively help you find the one that works best for you.

Values: I did not let him compromise my values yet again. One struggle was my value of family. It became a conflict as to whether I was to focus on my immediate family or my family of origin. I tried my best to balance both. Throughout the course of the relationship, I allowed him to compromise my values time and time again. I would set a hard boundary and he would walk right over it. Instead of ending things, or having a consequence for the boundary violation, I would take the boundary and move it further. He would cross it again over and over.

Do not let anyone else cause you to compromise your values. Living a value driven life can provide so much comfort, happiness, and satisfaction. Identify your core values and live a life consistent with them.

Shame Resilience: I was embarrassed and ashamed due to my husband's actions. I pushed through that shame and embarrassment by showing myself compassion.

Notice any shame or embarrassment you feel. Recognize it and then let it go. Treat yourself as you would treat a dear friend. You deserve it.

Responsibility: I did not take responsibility or blame for any of his actions. In the past, I had often tried to make it about me. To take responsibility some-how, because that felt easier than accepting that he was not who I thought he was. Trauma survivors frequently place blame on themselves. This is a trauma response and is a protective mechanism. If you can somehow blame yourself for what happened, then you can perhaps control it from happening again.

This is a false narrative. You are not responsible for what has happened to you. You are responsible for how you respond.

Chapter Seven:
Rock-a-Baby to Me

About a month after rehab, I joined the Army Reserve. Then some events unfolded leading to us securing an attorney in Texas in order for him to try and get custody of his 3 sons with the ex. It was a long, dramatic, and expensive ordeal. With the custody battle starting, I was forced to face reality. My husband had a baby with another woman and I was about to be raising him. The pain was significant and at times all consuming. I wanted my brain back, free of the pain of the situation. Whenever I would start to feel positive, loving feelings, my brain reminded me of all the pain.

On July 1, 2015 we drove to Texas and collected the boys. They were 11, 7, and 2 at the time. Our baby girl was about to turn 2. I knew I was about to be raising 6 kids and started to plan for it. We brought the boys home and began life as a family of 8. The little one called me "mommy" from that first day. I'll never know if he thought that was my name, or called me that because the baby did, or called me mommy because that's what I was to him. I bought a twin stroller. They wore the same size diapers. I bathed them together each night. I'd get them both dressed in their pajamas and they'd both crawl up in my lap in the rocking chair and we'd read 2 stories before bed. I loved this routine. They would say to me, "Mommy! Rock-a-baby to me!"(I used to sing "Rock-a-Bye Baby" to them in the rocking chair) The two of them were inseparable. They became the best of friends.

Our family did it's best to integrate. All of the kids had chores. I made charts of the chore rotation. The least desirable chore was the dishes. The most desirable spot in the car was the middle seat next to the two babies instead of in the far back, so the person who was on dish duty got to sit in the prime seat in the vehicle. The person with the easiest chore that week got the least favorite spot in the car. We had a list of family rules on the pantry door. We had a family calendar of who needed to be where and when. I had 8 laundry baskets, all with a child's name on the outside and two for the grownups. Laundry was an all-day affair. We had fun. We went to fun places and had many adventures. Christmas that year was my favorite to date. The entire front room was full of presents. The older 4 got bicycles. The babies got a play kitchen and wooden train table set. We had a great day.

Life as a family of 8 was not easy, but I loved it. Raising the little one was the most psychologically conflictual experience of my life. I loved him like he was mine, but at the same time his mere existence was soul-crushing as it was a constant reminder of the pain I had endured. I miss him to this day. I miss all 3 of them. The middle son and I had a special bond. He would draw me pictures at school and I'd hang them on the wall in my office. He knew he was my "favorite" and that he had a special place in my heart.

I was a football mom. All 4 of the older children, including my daughter, played tackle football. My husband was the coach. My daughter had been playing for several years at this point, and the strange looks I received from the team moms that fall when I showed up with 3 additional children, one the same age as my baby, was priceless. One had the courage to ask me about the additional 2-year-old. I looked her in the eye and said, "It's very complicated. My husband has made some mistakes, but this is my family. These are my children." I received a few high fives and a few said, "I don't know how you do it." Nothing was said after that.

In public, people would often ask if the babies were twins. Rather than explain, "No, actually the little boy is 5 months older. My husband cheated on me with his ex and got her pregnant and then I got pregnant with my daughter not knowing about him." I would just say yes.

I was not looking forward to the two of them starting school, being in the same grade, and having to explain how they weren't twins but were so close in age. I figured I would solve each problem as it came up. I knew the truth was the only solution, but there are various ways in which to tell the truth. My truth was, "My husband is a no good, lying, cheating, narcissistic womanizer who used me and his ex and got us both pregnant at the same time." That doesn't need to be my daughter's truth. Hers will be, "My dad isn't perfect, and he made some mistakes that hurt people. As a result, my brother and I are close in age." There is no benefit for me to disparage him to her. She is half of both of us. To disparage him is to disparage her. I will not do that.

I struggled with how to process everything. Below are some excerpts from my journal showing some of the pain, progression, and growth that took place over the course of several months.

October 16th 2015

I feel like I am inherently flawed and broken beyond repair. My therapist pointed out a theme in my life of finding myself in vulnerable positions.

I guess so.

It made me feel like a horrible person.

I think I have an internal image of myself as dirty and worthless. I don't deserve happiness or stability. I deserve pain, trauma and abuse.

My therapist is hopeful this can be overcome, but I see it as insurmountable because it's who I am. I feel like I'm not worthy of peace, calm and quiet.

I look to my husband to fill that void. Whenever his behavior is not transparent or consistent, I automatically go to why am I not enough? When he finally stops using for good or stops cheating, then it will mean I am good enough for somebody to love me unconditionally.

No one seems to have an answer for me as to how I can get past this. My options seem to be to toughen up or get out. I feel trapped. It feels unfair, but I made these choices. Now I have to choose how to deal with the consequences. I'm just so sick and tired of being miserable.

Part of me wants to throw myself into my military training and get that out of the way but it won't fill a void. The void seems unfillable. Like I'm too broken to be fixed. I felt broken my entire life. One bad thing after another has happened. Will I ever catch a break?

I need an answer, an answer to this endless suffering. An outlet to healing, wholeness and moving forward. Pretty much I only feel good when I feel like someone needs me and I'm helping them.

December 9th 2015

Today I read a journal from 7 years ago. So much about my life has changed during that time, but so much has remained the same, which is discouraging. So much pain has filled my life. I'm left wondering if I have experienced an abnormally large amount as compared to most people and have survived and thrived in spite of? Or have I experienced a normal level of pain and trauma and just get overwhelmed easily? Aside from childhood, much of the trauma has occurred in the past 7.5 years. It's time to re-write my story so the ending is brighter.

This is depressing, hurting all the time, not being able to experience joy and happiness for very long. The search for meaning and for answers has been ongoing for as long as I can remember.

Will I ever find what I'm looking for?

What I know for certain is I will never find answers or happiness in a man. It has to come from within. My struggle is not knowing exactly what that looks like or even how to make that happen.

Especially given the context of my marriage and current life situation. We've made it 2 years past the point of which our divorce would have made it been final if LegalZoom hadn't screwed up our paperwork. I've always believed that was a sign we were supposed to stay together.

Career wise, I would have stayed with the Bureau of Prisons and been miserable. I'm so glad I left. Best decision ever.

I feel unlovable and bad about myself. Like no one could ever love me long term after they got to know me, the real me. Being dumped sucks, but being cheated on sucks worse.

I struggle so much with feeling like I can never get better.

My relationships with family are damaged.

I hope I haven't totally screwed up my kids.

I have one failed marriage, and another that has been one train wreck after another.

I don't know what it is going to take for me to get better. I'm a psychologist for Christ's sake and I can't figure this out.

January 20th 2016

I'm not even sure where to begin. I want tomorrow with our marriage counselor to be productive. Getting clear on my emotions, my needs, my boundaries, I guess will be a good step. Every new hurt that comes up opens up old wounds wide open. I now have many regrets.

I regret not ending the relationship in August of 2010. I regret getting engaged so quickly, regret not ending it summer of 2011 when we were being evicted. Regret not trusting my gut out of fear. I would have been fine. Regret not ending in March 2013. Regret letting him come home. Not divorcing last year. All were fear-based decisions. I cannot live in fear. Fear of ruining my kids, fear of being alone, fear of failure, fear of struggle. I am strong, I can do this or anything I want to do.

Now I fantasize about life with just me and the kids. My client is struggling after reading 50 Shades of Grey *because she does not have that love in her life. I can relate because I loved my husband with everything that I had. I gave 100% of myself to him. I was vulnerable. He destroyed me. Destroyed my trust, my sense of safety in relationships. He reinforced the belief that no one has ever protected me, and no one ever will. Strangely he used to make me feel so special, so important and good enough. Then his actions made me feel like so much less. Not good enough, not special, not valued or cherished at all. I deserve to be valued and cherished by someone, and if I'm not, so what. I want to value and cherish myself.*

I have consistently set boundaries for myself and yet when he violates them. I let him off the hook. I've let him let me compromise my values time and time again. I've taught him how to treat me. I've allowed this to happen. No more. I will allow this no more. I don't know how best to proceed. My thoughts are, I tell him he can have the Honda, I will pay the phone and insurance, and we can develop a plan for where he will live or go. Then if my boundaries are violated again, we don't discuss, we just separate. I keep praying God will give me a sign and I'm either not seeing it or I'm choosing to hang on. The signs and feelings I've seen so far lead me to leaving. I want to get clear on what my needs are first, so I can feel secure in my decision making.

Sometimes I really missed the freedom I felt without my husband. I could come and go as I pleased and didn't have to feel anxious about it. I wish I knew why I feel so much guilt and anxiety when we aren't together. It's weird. My therapist pointed out yesterday something called a daemonic in existentialism. I guess it's when your strength crosses the boundary and becomes a deficit. So, me taking care of people is a strength but that I don't recognize the cost to myself. This lines up with the current lesson I'm working on in the Brene Brown class. We are examining the disconnect between our values and how we do or don't leave them out.

March 24th 2016

There are many negative situations in which I would respond hastily in the past in order to avoid pain. For example, I should have left my husband at least 10 times, but because I fear the pain of losing him, I stay.

Now it's no longer the pain of losing him but rather the kids. I don't want to hurt any of the kids, so I stay. In doing so I hurt myself on a daily basis because there is constant stimuli and reminders of all of the deceitful things he's done that have crushed my spirit over and over and over.

Most of me feels like I will not feel peace until after court, but then it will be something else and something else.

My goal is to learn how to stop living in a constant state of chaos and drama. I think I'm afraid of a peaceful life. I don't know what that feels like.

Trauma survivors function in chaos because it's familiar. I want a new familiar. A new normal.

I want to enjoy living my life rather than just surviving my life. I want to feel more balanced in my relationship by being able to trust him, not have to worry what he's spending his money on, if he's using, if he's cheating. But he never tells the truth.

Balance would be knowing he's faithful and honest with me and that he's changed. Balance would be being able to trust him to pay the bills he's responsible for, and knowing if I deploy, I won't come home to a foreclosed house and a repossessed car. Balance would be feeling loved wholeheartedly feeling genuinely appreciated and not feeling used. Balance would be having loving feelings towards him that I could confidently express without fears that he will hurt me again.

Honestly, as I write, occurs to me yet again how impossible this all feels. He is not the man I thought he was, and I'm not sure he ever can be. He's not willing to take a 100% honest inventory of his own life and history and dysfunction in order to change what he needs to in order to be a better person. I don't think I can provide the loving, supportive, accepting environment he needs in order to change. But if he's in an environment that lets him off the hook, he won't change. He will take advantage or take the easy way out.

For me, leaving is the easiest and most logical solution. But being a single mom is hard and I don't know if it is the best for the kids. I have no desire to ever be in another relationship again. I could never trust another human being again. Ever. So I would be facing life alone.

I want to grow old with someone and share life and travels together. But I just don't know if I can ever trust my husband enough for that. Once court is over, I have some more decisions to make, and so does he. Maybe I could make a list of what I need from him and see if it's possible for him to do it. I'm fine with him doing the same to see if I can incapable of fulfilling his needs. I'm not confident in my ability to do so anymore. I feel as if I've tried expressing this to him, but he says he just wants us to work.

We'll see, I guess. We've been in struggle nonstop for three years now. When will it end? When will it lighten up? I thought maybe having the boys was something that could help bring us together as a family, and in some ways, it has but in others it's made things harder. I wish God would give me a clear sign of what I'm supposed to do. I keep thinking court will determine it. If we keep the boys, then we are supposed to be a family. If we lose them then he and I are done. He will have nowhere to go and no resources. But I have to do what's best, whatever that is.

Climbing from Rock Bottom

My hope in sharing my journal entries, my struggle, my pain, is for you to see that it is okay to struggle. It is okay to question. It is okay to wonder why on Earth you are going through so many hard things.

One thing I had to search long and hard for was forgiveness and acceptance of MYSELF. I held myself responsible for much of the pain and suffering I had gone through. This is a common theme in childhood trauma survivors as children aren't able to make sense of the bad things that are happening to them, so they conclude that they must be to blame somehow. This had been my pattern throughout my life and I carried it well into adulthood.

I've said it before and I'll say it again, you are not what has happened to you! You are not responsible for all of the bad things that have happened in your life. No matter what, it is never too late to be who you were meant to be. Start today! Take an inventory of your life. Get rid of what isn't working and make changes that will allow you to move forward with peace and acceptance.

Footholds

Acceptance: I focused on accepting the situation. Acceptance allowed me to make it through each day. Acceptance empowered me to rise above all of the negative things I was saying to myself and elevate myself to a position of peace ultimately.

What can you accept that will allow you the freedom to move forward?

Love: I chose to love my stepson fully. It was hard. It hurt like hell, but he was a blessing. He brought more joy to my life than he did pain. As I mentioned earlier, he called me "Mommy" from the day we picked him up. I don't know if he thought I was his mommy, or if he thought that was my name. But I do know that I loved him fiercely and despite the pain surrounding his conception, he was a gift. He was my son. He will always take up space in my heart.

Love is a powerful antidote to pain. Love yourself. You deserve it.

Control: Control was a repeat foothold. In this particular situation I chose not to function in chaos. I chose to focus on what I could control. You do not have to continue to function in chaos just because it is familiar. You can choose to put order in your life, even in small ways. For many years I functioned in a constant state of chaos because that is what was familiar. Once one crisis ended, it seemed another would pop up. This is very common for trauma survivors. We function in chaos and uncertainty due to our brains being "stuck" in constant fight, flight or freeze mode.

It is okay to seize control of the chaos and focus bringing control and order to the parts of your life where you can effect change.

Chapter Eight:
Domestic Violence

I began to suspect my husband was using again. I wasn't sure how, but I had a feeling. I also began to suspect that he was using marijuana. It's legal in Colorado and he was no longer a Federal employee, so he could if he wanted to. My issue wasn't so much the drugs as it was the deceit that comes along with that. I questioned him. He denied it. I found residue in our bathroom. He said I was crazy. I let it go.

June 2016 – My childhood best friend, Susan, and her 4 sons moved from Ohio to live with us. She was fleeing a domestic violence situation and needed a fresh start. The day she called me in November of 2015 and told me that her husband had tried to kill her, I told her to get on a plane and come out. I'd take care of her. She had to wait until after the trial, so as soon as he was convicted and sentenced, she came.

She and her boys moved into my basement. We had 13 people, three adults and 10 kids, living in our house with three dogs and a bearded dragon. On my older daughter's 10th birthday, Susan and I took all of the kids to Dart Wars to celebrate. The kids had a great time shooting one another in a nerf gun battle. Susan and I talked about my concerns that my husband was using again.

We had his car that day, the SUV, because it fit everyone. When we pulled back in the driveway at home, I noticed something shoved between the seat and the center console. It was a blue envelope. I recognized my stepmom's handwriting and return address. The envelope was open. There was a birthday card inside for my daughter. It was the first one she received. She had commented earlier about how the whole family had forgotten her birthday. Usually, they send cards with cash. She hadn't received any.

Suddenly as I saw the open card it all made sense. I asked Susan to stay in the car after the kids got out. I was shaking. As soon as the last child exited the vehicle my shaking hand reached down and grabbed the envelope. It had a check in it made out to me for my daughter's birthday. I knew what had happened. My husband had been stealing the mail, opening her birthday cards and taking the cash. He couldn't do anything with this one because it was a check. I told Susan I was done. But I needed a plan to get him out of the house because I was scared. She said she'd help however she could.

June 28th 2016

So many mixed feelings and emotions. All of the times he has fucked up, I've contemplated ended things, but clearly haven't. Several people have commented how monotone I seem. Like I'm not sad, not angry, not anything really. I just am.

On Saturday I was prepared to file for divorce and not tell him until it was done. Then on Sunday he opened up a dialogue and I told him I found his steroids. The conversation progressed from there. He's heading back to rehab this weekend to try again. I don't have any of the feelings I had before. The fear. The trepidation. The uncertainty. I am not hopeful or optimistic either. I just AM. While he and the boys are gone, I'm going to focus on me and my kids. I will figure out what needs to happen for me to be happy, less angry, and maybe less forceful or dominant. Right now, I don't know.

I am driving him to Texas this weekend for rehab. He will be gone for 28 days and it's covered by insurance, which is a blessing. I am not sure what life is going to be like for me. Most everyone in my life is saying it's time to close up shop and move on. If only it were that simple.

Some of the things I look forward to if divorced: freedom, financial stress decreased, no longer being responsible for raising his love child. No stress about Marie. Closeness with my family again.

Disadvantages equal splitting up the family, hurting him and the boys. That's about all I can think of at this time.

What I need to do is remember that I am the only one who gets to make this decision. My parents and friends can have opinions, but it's my life and ultimately, he has hurt me so many times in awful ways. He does not deserve me. I do not deserve this. None of the kids deserve this either.

Other advantages to divorce: no phone tracking, no anxiety about what he's doing, who he's having sex with or what drugs he's using. No fears about missing money. So many things would change.

I would miss him though. He's always going to have a place in my heart, but he's very broken, and I'm very broken. Together we are a hot damn mess. I want things to be different. What do I want? I want commitment, 100% honesty, integrity, loyalty. I want open, honest communication. I want laughter, lightheartedness, good times, I want authenticity. I want him to be happy so the rest of us can be happy.

As I write all of this down it feels like a tall order. Like I don't know that he's capable of any of it. When he gets home, I guess we begin to figure things out. For better or for worse I made the commitment, but he didn't take it seriously. It's like it was all a joke to him. "Hey just kidding." He's been a piece of shit husband for our entire marriage. Most of me knows he's never going to change. This upcoming month will give me a chance to see what it's like to not have him around.

When I confronted him at first, per the usual, he denied everything and told me I was crazy. Then at some point he came clean, somewhat. He admitted he was using steroids again and smoking marijuana. I told him he needed treatment again. By this time, I had been in the Army for about a year and we had good health insurance, so I knew I could send him out of state for treatment. I suggested he find a treatment center in Texas and go there when he took the boys to their mom's house for the summer. He did. On July 1, 2016 Susan and I drove him and the boys to Texas. We dropped the boys off first, then my husband at a treatment center.

As soon as we got home, I met with an attorney and filed for divorce. I told the attorney I was scared. I didn't know what he'd do when he found out. He suggested I tell him while he was in rehab since he was surrounded with support and was far enough away, he couldn't get to me quickly. I did. He cried on the phone when I told him I had filed for divorce. He tried to leave rehab, but his sister convinced him to stay and get help.

July 11th 2016

Consider the person you want to be. What are three things you value? I am free, I am happy, I am content.

Where is the gap between where I am and where I want to be? With my husband gone there isn't much of a gap. With him here I feel trapped. I feel heavy discontent. I'm always on edge and on guard. I can be myself without him.

One step I can take is fill out the paperwork for the attorney and get it sent in. Another step I can take is telling him I don't want him to come home.

This go around with rehab is totally different. I don't miss him. I don't want him to come home. I see him as an entitled, narcissistic asshole. He manipulates me. He faked a suicide attempt. He doesn't give a shit about me at all.

I don't know why I'm so afraid to tell him I want to divorce. I stopped wearing my rings last week sometime. In my mind, it's already over. It's been over for a while now. I just need to pull the plug on everything, and soon. I don't want him coming home. I want my freedom. The peace of mind. I want to be happy.

A challenge that makes me feel stuck is ending my marriage. So many things have kept me engaged and stuck. Mostly I haven't wanted to hurt, and also, I didn't want to put the boys out.

But I deserve better. It's time for me to be free. It's time for me to live for only me, not him, and not for my kids. My life will never be fulfilled in this marriage. Trust has been violated too much. He's hurt me too many times, and he doesn't give a shit about anyone but himself. I need to be free. My life will begin once I tell him it's over. Not many people I know are stuck in my situation. I'm hoping he is reasonable. I can and do have the courage to tell him it's over.

I wasn't planning to let him come back home, but a week or so after I filed for divorce, he called and begged me to let him stay for a few weeks in order to find a place for him and the boys to go. If it wasn't for the boys, I would have said no. But I didn't want my boys to be homeless, so I agreed. Then we began an awkward month of me asking him daily if he had found a place, and him giving me bullshit answers and excuses. I just wanted a peaceful end to the entire ordeal. I wanted freedom.

On a Wednesday evening in August, he texted me that he was taking the boys to church. I said okay. Susan was home with my kids, and my friend had invited me over for dinner at his place to meet his girlfriend and her kids. He knew everything I was going through and said I needed a break. I turned off my phone and headed to his house.

At this point my husband was tracking my every move. To be fair, I was tracking his too. I had been for a while due to not trusting he was where he was supposed to be. We had developed an extremely unhealthy dance of mistrust and paranoia. I spent a few hours at my friend's house. He grilled steaks. I held the baby. I jumped on the trampoline with the other kids. I went home around 8.

Halfway home I turned my cellphone back on. It immediately began to chime with a host of missed calls and messages. "Where the fuck are you?" "Who the fuck are you with?" I was Facetiming a friend as I entered my house. I walked past my husband as he headed out the front door. I told my friend I was scared and that something was about to happen. I let him go. I put the babies to bed and then went into my bedroom to get ready for bed myself. I noticed the lock to my husband's handgun was on the bed. He had clearly gone somewhere with the gun. Then the text messages began.

He's going to go find my "friend." What is the address? What is his name? Why am I protecting him? How long have I been fucking him? I call my friend and tell him I am so sorry and that if my husband somehow finds his house, please don't answer the door, just call the police. He had 6 kids at the house including an infant. I told him to apologize to his girlfriend on my behalf and that I was terribly embarrassed to bring them into my drama. He said not to worry and that he had plenty of guns of his own.

I called one of my Army friends. She called the cops, and they came to the house. I told them everything that was going on. They told me I needed a restraining order. They said if he came home to call them. About an hour later he did. I ran to the basement and told Susan to call 911. She and her boys were terrified. I went back upstairs. He was furious. He tried to talk to me. I refused.

I went into my bathroom and locked the door. He forced himself in. He backed me into a corner and punched a hole in the wall just beside my head. I ducked and got out. I told him the cops were on their way. He removed his gun from his waist band and placed it under a pillow on the couch. He made sure I saw him do this. He wanted me to know he had a gun and he'd use it.

The cops came. It was the same three that were there prior that were so supportive and encouraging and telling me I needed a restraining order. While I'm talking to them, my husband comes out with his hands in the air. He told them he had a gun, and it was inside under a pillow on the couch and that they could search him. The cops separated the two of us. He told them what a controlling bitch I was and that I wouldn't let him have any money, I was cheating on him, etc. I laughed.

They told me to pay for a hotel for him for the night. I said, "I'd love to but he overdrew my checking account. I have -$879 right now."

The cops refused to make him leave. He said he won't leave without our daughter and there was no way I'd allow him to take her. We were at an impasse. I asked the cop if they could at least take his gun. His response was, "We can't interfere with his second amendment right to bear arms." My response: "Oh, so you're telling me you cannot help me. I have to sleep upstairs knowing he is below me with a gun under his pillow, and you can't do anything until he shoots me with it?" Cop: "That's correct ma'am."

I asked about the divorce papers and how it says that we are forbidden from disturbing the peace or threatening the other. The cop said, "So if you are wanting me to take him to jail, I am taking you for the same thing." Are you fucking serious?

Finally, the senior cop in the group talked to my husband and got him to agree to leave. He went in the house, grabbed a few things, and drove off. I then lost my shit on the cops. I told them I was an Officer in the US Army, a psychologist, a business owner, and I'd been in hellish relationship with this lying, conniving, cheating, stealing, narcissist for years and they just bought his bullshit story hook, line and sinker. They told me to call them if he returned.

I said, "With all due respect, FUCK YOU! I'll fight him myself before I call you for help. Why would I call you? So you can cart me off to jail? No thanks. I'll die first." I turned and marched toward my house. Halfway there I spun on heal and yelled, "You know he's right around the corner, don't you? He's going to start texting me as soon as he sees you drive away." I did an about face, then headed into the house.

Sure enough, 30 seconds after they pulled away, I get the texts.

Him: "Erica I'm sorry. Can I please just sleep on the couch tonight? I don't have anywhere to go. I promise I won't bother you. I don't want any more drama."

Me: "No".

Him: "Fuck you bitch! You are a worthless piece of shit." Etc, etc, etc."

I crawled into bed but didn't sleep. He returned early the next morning to get his boys ready and off to school. We didn't talk. Shortly after arriving at my office I got a call from my commander telling me I needed to report to his office at Fort Carson. I did.

He told me I had to meet with a Family Advocacy Program Social Worker and a domestic violence victim advocate. "What? Why? I don't need any help. I'm not a victim of domestic violence. I don't need the Army in my business." I was quickly informed that this was not optional and that my opinions were not necessary. He told me they were going to put me on orders for the following week, and were considering making me stay on-post so they could be sure I was safe.

I felt overwhelmed. I felt like I'd lost control of my own life. I felt like I was being punished. I felt like I was being backed into a corner. I met with the victim advocate. I told her I didn't think I needed to see her. That I wasn't a DV victim. She began to go through a checklist. Each question she asked, I answered yes to. Of all the questions the only two I answered "no" to were, "has he ever hit you" and "has he ever threatened to kill you?"

She explained to me that constant cheating, lying, threatening suicide, punching holes in walls, waving a gun around, threatening my coworkers, isolating me from friends and family, and accusing me of being crazy are all abusive behaviors, and that I was indeed a victim of domestic violence. I left feeling shocked. I wasn't sure how to absorb that information.

I didn't want that to be part of my identity. I had been victimized enough already. I didn't need one more "victim" title. I felt stupid. I felt little. I felt weak. What the hell was wrong with me? How did I let this happen? It all began to sink in. The dots were connected, the pieces fit together. He was never who he said he was. He was a chameleon. He changed himself to fit the situation and to get his needs met. When he met me, he met a paycheck. Well, his days of me as a paycheck were rapidly coming to an end.

August 4th 2016

To feel free, to be healthy, to be loved and cherished, to be wanted. These are all things I want and aspire to. I cannot get healthy in my marriage. I've been through too much. My heart has been repeatedly broken and I've been beaten down. I'm codependent with him and it's incredibly unhealthy.

What do I want my life to look like? I want to wake up happy, looking forward to my day. I want to be focused, centered, and present with clients. I want to sit in the living room with my kids and watch TV. I want to be at peace. I want to live my life feeling OK if I don't have a man. I don't want to be angry anymore. I want to travel with my kids. I want to provide them the best childhood possible. I can't do these things in my marriage. He is too unhealthy for it to be able to work.

My business will continue to be very successful. I will feel OK with myself. I value my freedom. He is a non-factor in my life now. I am no longer going to give him the satisfaction of knowing he has controlled me long enough.

It's time to be liberated, empowered. My life is complete without him. Breathe. I have done nothing wrong. I just need to put one foot in front of the other.

The military would not agree to let me go home unless I changed the locks on my house and kicked him out. I kept telling them I was more afraid of what he would do to me if he felt backed into a corner than I was to just let him stay a week or two longer until he found a job and a place to live. No one would listen to me. I agreed to do as I was told. I went to Lowe's and bought a new lock for the front door with a keycode entry. I changed the locks myself. I told him the Army wanted him out. He didn't believe me. I said he had seven days to find a place or he was sleeping in the car.

He found a place. I paid the security deposit and first month's rent at the advisement of my attorney. He said, "Erica it's worth it to get him out of the house. The judge would make you pay anyway because he has no income." So I did. I rented the moving van. The kids and I helped him and the boys pack and unload. He and I tried to be civil. We were for the most part.

August 23rd 2016

I am having random episodes of anxiety. It feels like out of nowhere this surge of panic washes over me. I just try my best to breathe through it. Right now, my biggest stressors are my divorce and getting him out of the house while trying to process and heal from an emotionally abusive marriage.

For years I have felt like I lost myself in this marriage and now it's time to find me again.

I'm coming to grips with the realization that I am a survivor of domestic abuse. I was reading up on gaslighting last night and that seems to be the main tactic he used. This is a hard pill to swallow. A hard identity to embrace.

A question I keep coming back to is why did I have to go through this struggle? What lesson am I supposed to learn in all of this? I am going to stop trying to control anything and everything around me. I am to let go and let God take control. There is a greater purpose for me on this earth.

When it came time to make decisions for the divorce in terms of division of property, assets and our daughter, I called him into the garage. "Listen. This is how this is going to go. You will not ask me for any of the equity in the house. You will not ask me for alimony. You can have your furniture and all of your belongings. You can have one of the TVs. You can have the Honda because it's paid for. I will keep the Tahoe since it's in my name. You can have the baby every other weekend. I will only ask for $50 a month in child support. You can agree to all of this, or I can make a call to an FBI agent to discuss your history of credit card theft, fraud, and identity theft. The statute of limitations has not run out."

He agreed to my terms. My attorney drafted the final divorce decree and several days later he and I went to my attorney's office and we both signed them. We just had to wait the remainder of the 90 days and it would be over.

September 7th 2016

The journey of less controlling has begun. It's time.

I've spent my entire life planning, predicting, micromanaging and trying to control every aspect of my life and environment. One thing I've learned from this is I cannot control others and I cannot make someone into something they aren't.

I have to accept and love people for who they are and allow them to control their own lives and learn from their own mistakes. I don't have to control whether or not a person falls in love with me. I can just be me. If someone doesn't fall in love that's OK. It doesn't mean I'm not worthy. It means I'm not the one for them.

It's OK to miss him. Missing him does not need to mean constant pain.

What I'm learning is pain ins"t that bad, and experiencing it allows it to fully process and go away. What I'm also learning lately is that setting boundaries feels good. It"s easy and remarkably feels better than the discomfort of doing something I don't want to do.

I am learning and growing from all of my experiences. I used to feel somewhat scared and almost sorry for myself and all I've been through and dealt with. This mindset is heavy and unproductive.

My life is what it is and happened because happened. Don't question it just go with it and move forward.

October 10th 2016

Army 10 miler yesterday! I killed it! I'm so very proud of myself and my time. Yesterday on the run, I had so much fun. It was an empowering and emotional experience to see my fellow brothers and sisters in arms missing limbs but running anyway - that was inspiring. I did a lot of self-reflection and thinking along the way. I wish I could somehow record my thought process to read when done. That would be pretty amazing.

Some of what I thought about along the way was how I've been lost for seven years. The last time I ran was the 2009 Big D Dallas half marathon. Running feeds my soul. When I'm running I can be 100% myself. I don't care about how I look, how I smell, or how I appear to others. It's just me and the road.

Looking back over the past seven years I realized I lost myself in the Bureau of prisons. Part of that was finding and marrying Michael. I ended up working for an agency full of evil and corruption. Lies, cheating, and stealing. Being made to feel like a sexual object each and every day by staff and inmates alike. It sucked the life out of me.

Then I had a home life that further depleted me rather than building me up. My children have always been my light. But they suffered too. They don't know what it's like to see their mom happy which is unfortunate.

Lately that has started to change. I have a career that is successful and feeds my spirit and soul. I am surrounded by friends and support. My military career is just beginning but I am proud to be a part of the army family and look forward to serving.

I realized somewhere along the route, that for all these years, I've sought validation from others. From my parents, my family, my employers, my coworkers, my community, but no matter how much I've achieved or accomplished I still felt somehow unworthy. Empty. Hollow.

*After leaving the Bureau of prisons and breaking free from the limita-
tions and expectations of the little box they put me in, I began to blos-
som and grow. Now I'm in a place in my life where I am seeing the results
of years of hard work and dedication.*

*The beauty of it all is realizing I don't need acceptance, validation, or
approval from anyone but myself. I am perfectly imperfect just the way
I am, and I don't need anyone else to confirm that.*

*I guess it took me training for three weeks and flying to DC to run the
army 10 miler by myself because it was something I wanted to do.*

*You see running has always been my escape, my lifeline. Over the past
six to seven years, I've allowed everything else to take priority and regular running was pushed aside. Along the route yesterday I was reminded
that running is my one true love. My go to. My sacred space. I didn't
realize how off track and lost I had become until somewhere around mile
7 of 10 I found myself again.*

*My steps became lighter my smile became brighter and I discovered for
the first time that I have within me all I will ever need. It just took me
awhile to find it.*

Climbing from Rock Bottom

I was finally empowered to live life for myself and no one else. It took my entire
adult life to arrive at the conclusion that I was worthy of being treated respect-
fully and didn't deserve constant abuse. I realized how much courage it took to
stand up to him and to maintain my boundaries. I focused on what I needed in
order to heal, and what my children needed as well. I had to realize that he was
not my responsibility. He had made choices and his choices had consequences.
He was responsible for dealing with those, not me. I also had to realize I was
ultimately not responsible for his boys. As much as I loved them, I couldn't stay
in an abusive marriage for them. I helped provide them a stable place to live and
groceries for the first few months out on their own until their dad could get on his
feet. I did not let them go without, but I knew I had to force him into taking control

of his own destiny, and I had to step away. It was very hard for me. But I did it. Remember? We can do hard things!

Footholds

Running: Running rejuvenates my spirit. Running feeds my soul.

Is there an activity that brings you joy and inspiration? If so, go do it! Any type of physical activity can help elevate mood and decrease anxiety. Yoga and meditation are both empirically supported to help with the physiological effects of PTSD. Many outdoor activities like hunting, fishing, camping, skiing, hiking, boating, etc., are not only beneficial due to the physical aspect, but also due to being outdoors.

Post-Traumatic Growth (PTG): PTG is a theory that explains the phenomenon of transformation after a traumatic event. My trauma taught me what I was made of and how strong I was.

Take a personal inventory of ways in which you have grown and changed after trauma. Without question you cannot go back to who you were before the trauma happened. Trauma changes you forever. That does not mean that you have to suffer negative effects for the rest of your life. Trauma can transform and facilitate growth.

Purpose: I focused on purpose. I wanted the pain I went through to serve a purpose somehow. I used my experiences to make me a better psychologist, a more understanding mother, a more patient friend.

You might have to look hard but try to find purpose and meaning in your struggle.

Chapter Nine:
Survival Mode

The next year and a half were a blur. I was in survival mode. The kids and I took a couple of cool vacations and road trips and enjoyed life as the Fantastic Four. We made it work, but was hard. I was always down and depressed. It was a struggle to get myself out of bed most days. The kids are the only thing that kept me going. I was barely present mentally. I did my best, but I found that many things would trigger my "fight or flight" response.

The slightest bit of stress would cause me to shut down. I experienced clinical depression, mood swings, explosive outbursts, overreactions, hyper alertness, irritability, anxiety, anger. Once I would become distressed it would take me a long time to calm down. I responded to innocuous situations as if they were life or death. I experienced sleep problems, sensitivity to noise, agitation, gastrointestinal distress, and hyper-vigilance (always being on "alert"). I experienced a great deal of shame at my lack of self-control over my irritability. I had difficulty concentrating on anything, difficulty focusing on the big picture instead of trauma triggers. I felt crazy because I couldn't always identify triggers for my symptoms. I was plagued by memory problems. I was numb. At times I used alcohol just to feel something besides shame, panic, and rage. I spent the better part of 2 years feeling detached, empty, apathetic, lethargic, mentally sluggish. Facing a trauma trigger felt like going to war. I didn't have the energy to parent. I felt like I was living in two different worlds: trauma plus present day.

One day, while talking to my teenage daughter, she shared some of her English class writings with me. One in particular was a paper on similes and metaphors. She wrote a metaphor about herself stating: "I am an ancient language that nobody understands." My heart broke for her knowing that she was struggling to fit in, to find her niche, find her place in this world.

She has been a unique, wonderful, beautiful, vibrant, energetic child since the day she was born. Our first memory together is of the day she was born. She was swaddled in a pink flowered blanket lying in my bed. She stared into my eyes like a wise old soul that I had known forever. I was overcome with gratitude and excitement at meeting the person I had waited for my whole life. I always wanted a daughter and now there she was. All of her uniqueness did not come without struggle. She has been hearing impaired since birth. Over time the hearing impairment became worse, resulting in hearing aids when she was in second grade. Her hearing impairment can cause misunderstandings in social situations if she isn't able to accurately hear what is being said to her, or what question she has been asked. She's embarrassed that she has to wear hearing aids.

My sweet, beautiful, spunky little June bug has always been a force to be reckoned with. She always has her own agenda, and if it doesn't match up with yours, well too bad. This created some power struggles during the toddler years, but we overcame. My mom used to always say to me, "I hope someday you have a daughter JUST like you." This was not meant as a compliment, but as a desire for me to understand how difficult it was to parent me at times. I certainly have a new appreciation for my parents.

In speaking with my daughter that day about her feelings that no one understood her, she continuously amazed me with her wisdom and maturity. We discussed her feelings and I explained to her that she might always struggle to find her "people" while she is in middle and high school. Being as smart as she is, as athletic as she is, as mature as she is, and to have overcome what she has been through, most people cannot relate to her. I explained to her that I struggled with similar feelings growing up.

I encouraged her to hang in there and to continue to be herself no matter what. She also shared a quote with me that she had come up with: "Be the light that guides people in the dark." She shared that some of her friends at school have described her as just that; the light that brightens someone's day and helps them get through tough times.

My daughter has certainly had her fair share of tough times. Our whole family has. During the period of survival mode, she wrote a rap song. My youngest was away for the night and I was preparing dinner for the crock pot for the following day. She asked if she could share her rap with me. I said of course. I continue chopping and dicing while listening. She began to rap about some of the struggles she has been through, all of which I knew about.

Then she gets to the age of 9 in the chronology of the rap. What she said next will indelibly be etched in my brain. My heart pounds and my palms sweat as I type this. I won't give the specific verbiage, as that is her story to tell. In essence my child, my angel, my bright light in the darkness had been sexually assaulted. As the room began to spin and I struggled to catch my breath, I continued to listen as she finished her rap. When she was done, I walked over and wrapped her in a huge hug. I asked her if she wanted to tell me what happened. She did. I reassured her she had done nothing wrong that I loved and supported her, and that we would get through this.

As I sat there in shock realizing that my worst nightmare had become my reality, I struggled to stay present. I remember having the feeling "I can never be happy again." I felt so many emotions: anger, sadness, hurt, guilt, shame, empathy, love. You see, I know what it's like to grow up with a secret. To always feel like you are "different" because of what has happened to you. To feel like you don't truly have any place that you fit in because no one else could possibly understand what you've been through, and you are too afraid to share for fear of what people will think.

My daughter was much braver than I. She spoke up. She told me what happened, and while I couldn't protect her at the time, I would be right beside her as she healed. I didn't do that when I was young. I told a friend once when I was in eighth grade. Then kept the secret until college when I finally reached out for help. I never wanted my story to become my daughter's story. I didn't want her to have a life of fear, anxiety, self-loathing and self-hatred. I didn't want her to feel shame. I didn't want her to constantly find herself in a string of abusive and/or dysfunctional relationships because she didn't feel worthy of being loved and treated well. I didn't want her to sabotage herself over and over again. Yet there we were.

The following several days were a blur of phone calls to CPS, the police, speaking with detectives, forensic interviews, SANE exams, and countless phone calls and text messages with the few friends I chose to lean on for support. I'd been through hell in the past, but the morning of May 23, 2018 was the hardest morning I've ever had. Just to swing my legs over the side of the bed and take those first steps, knowing that my baby was never going to be the same, and that the day would be hectic and overwhelming for us both.

I cannot describe the darkness, the depression, the hopelessness and horror. I would have given anything, ANYTHING, to trade places with her. To give her her freedom and innocence again. She was brave and courageous through it all. Every step of the way she held her head high and faced whatever challenge was put in front of her. She answered questions and endured exams. She was heroic. I tried my best to show the appropriate amount of care and concern while hiding how devastated I was and how hard it was to function. But I put one foot in front of the other and encouraged her to do the same. I surrounded her with love, support, resources, and tried my best to give her hope.

My kids know what happened to me as a kid. They don't know details, but they know something terrible happened. My daughter said to me during her ordeal, "Mom I feel sad for you that you had no one to support you like I do." I reassured her I am fine and that I'll do everything in my power to be sure she is fine too. Her bravery and courageousness inspired me to reach out to my own mom to not only tell her what had happened to my daughter, but to explain how triggering it was for me because of my own childhood. My mom was shocked and upset by both scenarios. She had no idea what I had been through as a kid. She felt she had failed me as a mother. I assured her she hadn't. What I've been through has made me who I am, and I don't know that I'd change anything.

My daughter holds her head high and walks with purpose and courage, but I know she struggles. I know she struggles to make sense of it all. Struggles to find meaning and purpose in it all. She is by far the strongest person I know. She works hard, and "quit" isn't in her vocabulary. I love this kid beyond words and am so proud to be her mom. My hope for her is that through her strength and determination, she will recognize that she doesn't have to go it alone.

She and I have discussed this many times. We talked frequently in the beginning, but as time passes, I struggle to find balance between talking about it "too much" or "not enough." I don't want her to feel like this has become her identity and that she'll never recover. I also don't want her to feel like because we aren't talking about it, that I don't care or that I expect her to have "moved on." I try my best to let her know that she can come to me any time, and that she'll always have my ear.

We've discussed writing a book together. This is another area in which my love for this child cannot even be described in words. Through her pain and struggle she wants to tell her story so that she can help other girls. I discussed this chapter with her and read it to her to see what her thoughts were and agreed to just delete it altogether if she didn't want me to write about her story. She said she loved it and was excited for it to help people.

During the time following her disclosure I searched and searched for resources that would help me. Resources that would tell me what to do and perhaps how to feel. I found a dearth of information. There is plenty of research that tells me what the risks are of childhood sexual assault and abuse in terms of long-term development. I wanted information on how to prevent that.

I was introduced to KidPower, a local non-profit that helps kids learn communication and self-defense skills to help feel empowered in the event they are attacked or approached by a familiar or unfamiliar individual and are uncomfortable. My daughter reluctantly participated but got a lot out of the experience.

I found a parent support group. The group was closed, structured, and curriculum-based. I found myself feeling very pissed-off each week. I did not participate, I sat and listened. I felt self-conscious that there I was, a licensed psychologist needing help because her child had been sexually abused.

It took several weeks for me to feel comfortable enough to participate. After one group activity in which we were tasked with choosing two photos, one that represented how we felt now, and how we hoped to feel at the end of the group. I volunteered to share. My first photo was chaotic and out of control symbolizing perfectly how I felt on the inside. The second picture was of a woman in a lotus position appearing to meditate near a calm body of water.

As I shared my anger and my frustration, something shifted in me. I cannot describe exactly what happened, but for me verbalizing my anger took away its power. Instead, it empowered me to move forward without the heavy burden of carrying that much anger and hostility.

The fall of 2018 brought with it the confirmation hearing of Brett Cavanaugh to the US Supreme Court as well as a rise in the #metoo movement founded by activist Turana Burke. My daughter and I had great conversations about what this movement meant and the potential to give abuse survivors a voice.

Each year I try to run the Army 10-miler in Washington, D.C. In 2018, I took my older two children with me. We were able to see protests at the Capital building and on the steps of the Supreme Court calling for Brett Cavanaugh to not be confirmed. My children were able to witness and be a part of history. On that trip we also visited the Holocaust Museum which sparked an interest for my daughter in WWII history. My children and I discussed the importance of standing up for what is right despite any opposition you may receive. My daughter and I discussed how well-behaved women don't make history, and that sometimes that means being vocal and taking actions in ways that buck against societal norms.

I hate that the two of us are both members of the #metoo movement as survivors, but at the same time I am proud of the strength and resilience of my daughter and the millions of other women in the movement that had the courage to come forward and say, "me too".

Climbing from Rock Bottom

To this day, my true rock bottom was learning that my daughter had been sexually assaulted. Everything I had gone through prior to that point paled in comparison to what it was like to feel completely and utterly helpless. It was my worst nightmare come true. I never wanted my children to have to struggle and suffer the way I did. I wanted to take her pain away. To somehow make it all better. But I couldn't. The best I could do was be by her side, be strong and courageous, and to be sure she received everything she needed in order to heal.

As parents I think it often pains us more to see our children struggle than it does to struggle ourselves. We often to strive to make their lives easier, to prevent them from feeling pain, disappointment, or discouragement. What I've learned over time is that we cannot prevent all bad things from happening to our children. Despite our best-efforts life still happens.

I've also learned over time in my clinical work that children who go through hard things as kids with proper support and resources, go on to be strong, resilient adults and are better equipped to deal with the hardships of life than children with minimal struggle. While this did not make me feel any better as my daughter was struggling, it did help me to focus on getting her help and resources and doing my best to minimize the potential long-term damage of her trauma.

I believed my daughter. I never once questioned anything about her story. I left it to the professionals to determine the best course of action as far as the perpetrator and focused my energy on protecting her from the process and the system that likes to blame victims. We were fortunate in that from the police officer that took the initial report, to the forensic investigator, the medical examiner, the detective, the prosecutor, and the judge all believed my daughter. She did not experience any shame or victim blaming at the hands of the professionals in her case. She did experience shame and self-blame but has fortunately been able to work through a good bit of that in therapy.

Her road to healing and recovery will be life long, but my hope is we set her up for success and put her on the right path moving forward.

Footholds

Justice: I struggled as a mother when reporting my daughter's assault. I wanted to shield her from the reporting process, and the court process. I didn't want her to experience victim blaming. We were so fortunate that the detective on the case was amazing. Justice was served. Her assailant took a plea deal and completed sex offender treatment and probation. My daughter was supported every step of the way and did not get revictimized by the system.

You deserve justice. You are not what has happened to you. Fight to be heard. Fight to have a voice. Don't let the system determine your validity and your worth. Find an advocate that can help you navigate any processes or procedures you must go through.

My Daughter: She likely had no idea, but she helped me through this tragedy just as much as I helped her. Her courage, her strength, her resilience, her "can do" attitude, her desire and willingness to help others made me put one foot in front of the other and do what was necessary to bring her justice and get her help. She was my "why" (and still is). She approached me not long after the investigation wrapped up and stated she wanted to write a book with me to help other girls and families heal from the trauma of sexual violence and abuse. There isn't a doubt in my mind that she will do just that. I found strength in her as I helped her navigate this awful situation.

Find strength in those around you even if you have to dig deep to move forward.

Support. I was so angry. So, so, so angry. For many months I carried that anger around like giant anvil. Finding a parent support group made all the difference. I was able to release the anger and begin healing.

Search for a support group. Facebook has many groups dedicated to various causes/illnesses/events. A simple Google search can often connect you with others that share your struggles. There is strength and healing in the camaraderie that comes with surviving trauma.

Chapter Ten:
Deployment

"I am a part of all that I have met; yet all experience is an arch where through gleams that untraveled world forever and forever as I move." - Alfred Lord Tennyson

I grew up in and around firehouses, firefighters, nurses and emergency rooms. My parents were both first responders. When people were in their worst moments, my parents were right there beside them fighting for their lives. Whether it was pulling someone from a burning building, extracting someone from a mangled car, or stopping bleeding and starting a heart, there was no hesitation to jump in and do what needed to be done. I wanted to be just like them, however blood and injuries make me faint.

I don't have what it takes to do those jobs. I used to feel "less than" as a result: Like I was broken somehow, or a disappointment because I couldn't carry on the legacy. However, as I reflect back, I remember being drawn to folks who were hurting psychologically even as a child.

Once, when I was an elementary school student, my step-grandmother came to pick me up from gymnastics because my mom had responded to a car accident (she was a volunteer EMT) and couldn't retrieve me. My grandma dropped me off in the emergency room of one of our local hospitals. I remember the somewhat chaotic scene of ambulances and stretchers, but what stood out were the individuals surrounding me in the waiting room.

I observed the families that were waiting to hear the status of a loved one. I remember watching my tall, graceful, beautiful mother be approached by a group of family members asking about one of the individuals in the accident. My mom, with compassion and grace, told the family that one of the passengers didn't make it. I still remember his name, even though I didn't know him or his family. I remember the wails of anguish and the collapse of one of the family members as the news hit them like a giant anvil. I was drawn to them. I wanted to sit with them and somehow make it better.

Flash forward 28 years and it has finally occurred to me that I have the same desire to help and heal people as my parents did. In many ways, I'm a psychological first responder. Perhaps I was a service dog in a former life because I just want to be near people when they are hurting. I want to be the person that takes the pain away and helps them turn it into something they can learn and grow from if at all possible. When people are in their darkest moments, I am there to hold their pain with them, reassure them that their response to the situation is normal, and that it's okay to feel whatever it is they are feeling. I validate them. I acknowledge them. I hear them. It has occurred to me that I am in a position to save lives just like my mom and dad.

In November, 2018, I received orders to deploy as a clinical psychologist with a combat operational stress control unit. I experienced a whirlwind of emotions over the first 24 hours. I was excited. I was scared. I was sad. I was anxious. What would happen to my business? What would I do with my kids? Would they be okay? What if I didn't come home to them? What would happen then? Could I do this job? Would I be effective? Would I be helpful? I entered planning mode and began to take care of the details.

From January to late March of 2019, there was a flurry of travel, training, and preparation. I made arrangements for my practice, my kids, my financial affairs, etc. On March 28, 2019 I hugged my kids for what I hoped would not be the last time and boarded a flight to Seattle to join the rest of my unit.

During deployment, I didn't sustain any significant traumas, but I sat with hundreds of service members that had. At the end of every day, I tried to take a deep breath and shake off all of the traumas that have attached themselves to me throughout the day as I helped service members sift through and unpack their emotions. But despite my best efforts, I kept a little piece of each service member, each person I helped, with me. They became a part of me. They became a tiny part of my story because I've become a part of theirs. During deployment I finally made time to begin writing. All of the traumas I had experienced over the previous decade came cascading out in the form of a blog. *Chasing the Sunset* became my therapy. Writing blog posts was my way to begin healing from all that I had stuffed away for so many years.

During one particularly draining week I sat with not one, not two, not three, but four female soldiers all individually impacted by sexual assault. These women did not know me. They did not know one another. Their stories were different, yet their stories were the same. Their stories have been told by thousands of women over thousands of years. How could I continue to sit in those moments and hold their trauma and their grief in my hands knowing the pain was caused by our brothers in arms? How could I help heal the brokenness caused by betrayal of trust and violation of some of the deepest, most sacred boundaries?

The answer was not simple. I sat with them. I held their grief with them in that moment, being completely and totally present. I believed in them. I walked with them hand in hand as they began a journey towards healing.

I AM a part of all that I have met.

As my deployment drew to a close, I found myself pondering the level of impact I'd made. For as long as I can remember I've loved helping people and I've loved being a leader. The deployment had placed me in a position to be and do both. I didn't have much time for writing the final few months due to being placed in a leadership role. No. That statement is not accurate. I'd had time to write. I just hadn't had the mental energy to do it. But I'd had several service members thank me for saving their lives on the deployment. Yet, I didn't stop any bleeding. I didn't sew any wounds. I didn't do CPR. I listened. I was present. I cared. I showed up.

Some days I wonder how it is that I am 41 years old. Life seems to have gone by in the blink of an eye. Then I stop and ponder the path I've been on, the twists, the turns, the detours, the bumpy roads, the smooth sailing. I have been blessed with more adventures and experiences in my short 41 years than many individuals get in one lifetime. The flip side is experiencing more trauma, pain, and heartbreak than most as well.

The quote at the beginning of the chapter has been my favorite since my senior year English class. At the time, I did not realize the truth that would ring forth for me in those words, yet here I am. I am a part of all that I have met. Each person that I have encountered whether it be personally or professionally, has had an impact on my life. Each experience, both positive and negative, has impacted and shaped my steps.

As I move, the world becomes a smaller place. One foot in front of the other, I encounter new people, new experiences, new joys and new pains.

Climbing from Rock Bottom

Typically, on long runs, especially races, I feel inspired with various stories and ideas. Running recharges my batteries. One Saturday in December during my deployment, I was hoping to feel inspired. I was running a half marathon on one of the world's longest bridges on a beautiful warm and sunny day in Kuwait. However, anxiety, worry, and stomach upset derailed my typical mental inspiration. What I did notice was the mental battle with myself. It was like an internal argument.

One part of me was criticizing myself for not training harder, not making myself more of a priority, for letting other people get in my head and make me feel "less than." The other part of me was saying, "Get it together Erica. You've got this! Who cares if you have to crawl across the finish line? At least you finished." Interestingly enough, I'm beginning to see the metaphor between that day's race and my experiences on my deployment.

When I signed up for the race, I was excited, nervous, motivated, and enthusiastic. I had time goals I wanted to accomplish and I knew I could do it. My training didn't go as planned for a variety of reasons. Late nights at the clinic combined with poor sleep often resulted in skipped workouts. Despite knowing that I carried the burdens of the day on my shoulders and running helped me process and shed those, I just wanted to crawl into my bunk and mentally check out.

Fortunately for me I had accumulated quite a few miles over the course of the previous nine months, and it carried me to the finish line over 30 minutes slower than I know I'm capable of. I had a choice to make regarding how I would feel. I could choose to be down, depressed, and disappointed in myself, feeling like a failure, or I could accept what the race gave me and be proud of myself for making it to the finish line. I chose the latter.

Similar to my race experience, I began the deployment with many grand plans and goals of things I wanted to do while I was away. I wanted to run x number of miles, read x number of books, write in my journal every day, start and finish writing my book, "find" myself again, etc. Much like my race training, my intentions were good.

However, life happened, and I didn't make as much progress on certain goals as I would have liked. I found myself nearing the end with a choice to make. Should I focus on all of the things I didn't do, or didn't finish, or the times I struggled and wasn't my best self? Or should I choose to see myself, and my experience as a success? It was an easy choice. I chose success.

For every time things didn't go as planned, for every goal that wasn't achieved, for every run that I missed, there were twice as many soldiers that felt heard, validated, acknowledged and understood. Soldiers that will hopefully, be better as a result.

Footholds

Running: I've mentioned it before, it's where I process my struggles.

Find a physical activity that helps alleviate your stress such as running, walking, yoga, weight lifting, hiking, biking, etc.

Therapy: Therapy has changed my life. My healing journey began a long, long time ago, and has continued ever since. I have never been ashamed to see a therapist. I find great healing in sharing my story with a trained professional to help me through. Even today I see my psychologist on a bi-weekly basis to maintain the growth and healing I've achieved.

Please find a professional to help you through your healing. You do not have to do this alone. While I did not see a therapist while I was deployed, I was in a unit full of other behavioral health professionals. We all leaned on one another for support during difficult times. We all carried the burdens of the soldiers we treated. As therapists we helped soldiers stay mission ready and helped them to process the burdens and traumas of the deployment in hopes they would have an easier time acclimating when they got home.

Reframing: The process of choosing to see my successes versus my failures is what we call "reframing." Taking a situation and finding an alternative way of interpreting it can have tremendous benefit.

Ask yourself if there is another way you can view the situation. It isn't about making a negative situation positive. It is about finding balance.

Chapter Eleven:
Naked in the DFAC

Since I started my blog during deployment, I noticed myself writing posts in my head all day long. This was good for me as it forced me to finally get my stories and ideas down on "paper." This book was slowly being formulated in my mind, one story at a time. For years I have felt like I had to start at the beginning and write until the end in chronological order. Then I realized many authors start somewhere in the middle and build from there. So that's what I did.

The process has been very dichotomous so far. On the one hand sharing my stories and struggles is very healing and liberating, and on the other it's very scary and I feel vulnerable. The best analogy I can think of is it's like walking naked in the DFAC (dinning facility) during dinner rush.

The first time I walk in with no clothes on, and everyone stops what they are doing, turns and stares. Some will wonder, "What the hell is she doing?" Others will snicker and point. Some may even take that opportunity to say something mean, hateful, degrading, or inappropriate, thinking that because I am naked and vulnerable, I have willingly opened myself to criticism. The first time I enter I'm feeling terrified, exposed, frightened and vulnerable, yet I walk boldly in, ignoring the reactions around me. I grab my tray, wait in line for my food, then go sit down and eat my dinner.

The next time I walk in naked my routine remains the same, but I am more confident, I feel freer, more liberated. The reactions are very similar from those in the

DFAC. Some are shocked. Some feel bad for me that I am there with no clothes on. Some give me a "high five" and say, "You go girl! Be bold! Be brave! Be free!" Some simply choose to ignore me because I am not relevant.

By the third time, and during subsequent times, I am walking through the DFAC boldly with a smile on my face. I'm comfortable and calm. I make eye contact and smile at folks. By the end of the week, people think, "There's the naked chick again. She's pretty bold and brave to come in here with no clothes on (or stupid depending on your perspective)." They continue with their dinner. It might even inspire someone else to live boldly, take their clothes off, and enter the DFAC. Or maybe they choose to just remove an article of clothing, or a layer. My boldness has helped increase their confidence that they too can face the critics in the DFAC.

I am the same me when I enter the DFAC each time. The reactions might be painful or upsetting but at the end of the meal, I leave, and guess what? I'm still the same me. The feelings, thoughts, and reactions of others only impact me if I allow them to. I can imagine that I have a Teflon skin and that whatever is said to me slides right off. I can choose to take in the praise and positive feedback, consider the constructive feedback as it helps me improve, and discard the negative and hurtful feedback as it isn't helpful and is only true if I allow it to be.

To be clear this is not about nudity. I am not advocating for anyone to march into the DFAC without clothing. I am advocating for vulnerability. Brene Brown in her best-selling book *Daring Greatly: How the Courage to Be Vulnerable Transforms the Way We Live, Love, Parent, and Lead,* quotes Theodore Roosevelt's speech "Citizenship of the Republic":

> *"It is not the critic who counts; not the man who points out how the strong man stumbles, or where the doer of deeds could have done them better.*
>
> *The credit belongs to the man who is actually in the arena, whose face is marred by dust and sweat and blood; who strives valiantly; who errs, who comes short again, and again,*

Because there is no effort without error and shortcoming; but who does actually strive to do the deeds; who knows great enthusiasms, the great devotions; who spends himself in a worthy cause;

Who at the best knows in the end the triumph of high achievement, and who at the worst, if he fails, at least fails while daring greatly."

I'd like to think I'm choosing to "dare greatly." In fact, after my very first blog post, a friend texted me something along those lines.

Brene Brown is someone I look up to and admire. Her work has helped me through some very tough times. Her book *Rising Strong* is about getting back up and dusting yourself off when you fall. I've done that time and time again. So much so that it makes it hard to imagine a life without constant struggle and trauma. This is typical for someone with a trauma history, to struggle to see a light at the end of the tunnel, to feel that survival is synonymous with living. I see it every single day in the faces and stories of my clients. I used to feel it every single day as I put one foot in front of the other. Lately I've felt different, lighter, freer, more liberated just like the naked girl in the DFAC.

So, for those of you that feel scared, naked, vulnerable, broken, and beat down, I encourage you to stand tall, walk boldly into that DFAC, grab your tray, get your food, and proudly and confidently find a place to sit and enjoy your meal. It's time to start living. Who needs clothes in the DFAC anyway?

Footholds

Vulnerability: Choosing to tell my story in a very public way made me feel very vulnerable. Like I was naked in front of millions of people. Being vulnerable is scary, but it can also be deeply rewarding.

Courage: Being vulnerable takes courage. I felt supported and encouraged by friends and family. This helped to find the courage to take that leap. Be courageous my friend!

Boldness: Be brave, be bold, be free. I have found that setting aside the thoughts and opinions of others in order to be bold and authentic is very liberating.

Don't be afraid. Be bold, be brave, be FREE!

Chapter Twelve:
Coming Home

I didn't expect it to be this hard. Part of my job during deployment was to give "redeployment" briefs to soldiers preparing to return home. We talked about the reintegration process, ways it might be difficult, ways to prepare yourself and your family, where to get help if it got too hard. I wrongly assumed that because I was a psychologist with knowledge about reintegration, it would be easy for me. I also wrongly believed that because I was not in "combat," my reintegration would be easy. Sadly, I was mistaken.

I returned home on January 29, 2020. Less than 6 weeks later the world shut down due to COVID-19. During those first weeks home, I enjoyed being with my children and with my mom and pets, but I was only comfortable at home. I found myself unable to go to the grocery store, unable to leave the house other than to take the kids to school, uninterested in seeing friends or family outside of my home. I felt like a square peg in a round hole. Why didn't I fit in anymore? Where was the Erica that left on March 28, 2019? Had I really changed that much?

I struggled to sleep, struggled to relax, struggled to find the motivation to return to the work I love. I felt numb. I felt like the world had gone on without me for 10+ months and now I was trying to find my way back into it.

I missed the soldiers I had deployed with. I yearned to be near someone that understood what I was going through. Someone that felt what I was feeling. Was I broken? Did anyone else feel this way? Was anyone else struggling with being home? I hesitated to reach out to anyone as I knew they were spending time with family and friends and getting reintegrated themselves. I didn't want to burden anyone else with my struggles. Was I weak? Why couldn't I just be "normal" again?

Dr. Dan Siegel came up with the concept of a "window of tolerance." Essentially, we each have a "window of tolerance" that governs our body's response to adverse stimuli. Individuals with a trauma history tend to have a small window of tolerance. We either function above the window, being hyper-aroused, jumpy, irritable, easily startled, easily angered, anxious, difficulty sleeping, etc., or we function below the window, being numb, slow, depressed, checked-out, unmotivated, etc. This is an incredible simplified explanation to an important and powerful concept, but I do so for brevity.

Several weeks prior to the end of our deployment I could feel myself slipping further and further below the window of tolerance. We were facing an increased threat from a nearby adversary. This caused us to go into a higher level of security precaution. As the threat level increased, so did my anxiety. It wasn't that I was afraid to die. I don't know that I ever have been. I was afraid of never returning to my children. I was afraid that the March 28, 2019 was the last time I was ever going to wrap them up in a big "mom" hug. I was afraid that the world was becoming a very scary place and that I would not be there to protect them.

We were informed that due to the increase in threat, our plans to return home would likely be altered. There was a very real possibility that our deployment would be extended. Depending on what happened, that extension could have been indefinite.

As all of this happened, I felt myself shutting down more and more. At times it was hard to speak. My movements slowed, my speech slowed, my sleep was non-existent. I withdrew from contacting family and friends. All I wanted was to go home to my kids and my greatest fear was that not happening. I wanted the world to be a peaceful, safe place so that no more American Service Members would lose their lives or return home broken beyond repair. I wanted the world to be safe for my children, and my children's children. I felt powerless and paralyzed, yet I still had a job to do.

Fortunately, I did (and do) have an amazing support team of my own. My psychologist saw me within a week of me being home. My naturopath also saw me within a few short weeks. Both said to me, "Erica, of course you are struggling! What you went through was hard." Each time either of them would reiterate this, I would feel a little weight leave my shoulders. As I would tell the soldiers during redeployment briefings, "It takes time! Be patient with yourself and with your family!"

Sometimes I struggle to practice what I preach, or to remember that I am a human being that responds as other human beings do. I tried my best to return to my old routines, but I still felt paralyzed. I didn't want to go for a run. I didn't want to see anyone. I didn't want to read or write. I just wanted to checkout and disconnect.

Here we are, many months later. I am happy to report I am feeling much better. I no longer fear leaving the house. I no longer avoid friends and family. I have been back at work full time for several months now and find myself getting back into a groove. Although I have hit a bit of a snag lately, I've been in the gym nearly every day since it re-opened. I am trying to put my health first, and to be patient with myself.

Am I back to the old Erica? No. I don't think I ever will be. One cannot deploy for 9+ months and return home the same person they were before they left. The experience changes you. It changes your worldview. It changes and shapes your goals and dreams. It reminds you of what it feels like to hit rock bottom with nothing to rely on but your knowledge and bad-assery. It reminds you that you are loved and supported beyond measure, but that reaching out and asking for help feels harder than marching head-on into a war zone.

It reminds you that rock bottom is where bad bitches are built.

Footholds

Reading: Glennon Doyle's *Untamed*, Brene Brown's *The Gifts of Imperfection, Rising Strong, Daring Greatly*, Writings by Sue Monk Kid.

Reading books by strong female authors helped empower me to move forward. Take a look at the reading list in the "Resources" section. These women picked me up and put me back on my feet.

Podcasts: The *Unlocking Us Podcast* by Brene Brown has rejuvenated me. Check it out!

Therapy: Within days of being home I was sitting in the office of my psychologist. As I explained to her all of the hard things from the deployment and how I was not reintegrating well, she held my pain and struggle and affirmed and validated my experience. I cannot stress enough the importance of professional help.

Chapter Thirteen:
Charlie Mike

Trauma is what drew me to the mental health field, but the irony is, the vast majority of the trauma I've experienced in my life came AFTER I was licensed as a psychologist.

I have learned several major lessons over the past 10+ years. I've learned that I am a human being that responds to trauma and stress the way every human is biologically hardwired to do so. I've learned that my childhood trauma history impacted my self-esteem, self-worth, and ability to clearly recognize dysfunctional patterns of behavior in romantic relationships. As mentioned before, I just wanted to be loved! The desire to be loved is a basic human need, and we all desire connection with other humans.

I've learned that I am tougher than I thought and that I can overcome any hurdle or challenge that is set in front of me. I've learned that the traumas I've experienced have provided me with knowledge, wisdom, awareness, skills, and abilities that allow me to effectively help others that experience trauma. I've learned that just because I am a psychologist does not mean I am immune to the devastation life's traumas inflict. I've learned that being vulnerable is one of the most courageous acts a human can engage in. I've learned that no matter what, I can rise up the next day and put one foot in front of the other, and I will eventually arrive at a resolution or find peace and comfort.

In the military we use a great deal of acronyms. Charlie Mike is military lingo for "continue mission." During combat, things do not always go as planned. Soldiers and leaders need to be prepared to change course and direction on a moment's notice. They need to be flexible. They also need to be able to continue the mission despite failure, despite loss of resources, and loss of life. As a psychologist, similar principles apply. One might have a plan for how to help someone, only to have to rapidly shift course if the original plan isn't working. The sample principle applies though, one must continue the mission.

As a human being I have experienced indescribable traumas. As a psychologist I have witnessed and heard about indescribable traumas. No matter what is put in front of me I will always Charlie Mike.

My mission in writing this book is to empower and encourage YOU the reader to know your worth. To know your ability to heal, and to know you are not what has happened to you.

I want you to know that you are absolutely not alone in this journey. My mission is to show you that all humans, even licensed psychologists, experience pain, trauma and hardship, but have the amazing capacity for tremendous healing and post traumatic growth. My mission is for you to understand that being vulnerable is not a sign of weakness, but of great courage and strength. Being vulnerable is necessary to grow, to heal, and to experience all of the richness life has to offer.

I want you to know you are brave! You are courageous! You have absolutely everything it takes to heal. You are worthy of love, belonging, care and compassion. You deserve to be treated like the unique, precious gift that you are. Your life is now. Right now. In this very moment. Now go live! Be brave! Be bold! Be free!

Afterward

Let me make one thing clear: This book is not about my ex-husband. It is not meant to vilify him or speak ill of him. He is a human being with his own struggles. I hated him for several years, but that hate was eating me up inside. I had to let go of it. All of the things he did to me were never about me. They were about him. They were about his dysfunction and his desire to meet his own needs by any means possible without regard for the impact on others.

I have forgiven myself. Finally. All I wanted was a family, someone to love that would love me back with the same fierceness and intensity that I bring to a relationship. Someone that would put up with my mood swings and my trauma history. I thought I had found that. The truth is, he was never who I thought he was. Like I said, he sold me a story and I bought it. I failed to act on the red flags because they did not fit the narrative I wanted for myself.

This book is a product of my healing journey, chronicled in hopes others can benefit from reading what it was like to climb up from rock bottom.

Acknowledgments

It's hard to decide where to begin. So many individuals played an integral part in my story. I'd like to begin by thanking my parents. I didn't come with an instruction manual and you did a great a job. Thank you for always supporting me even when you didn't understand what I was doing.

To my brother TJ: without you I wouldn't be me. You were the first person I took charge of, cared for, and tried to control. Thanks for still loving me despite how bossy I was.

To Conner, Avery, and Amaya: thank you for being the reason I breathe. The three of you have brought so much joy and love to my life even in the midst of the darkest times. We will always be the Fantastic Four. I love you in the back of the moon.

To my tribe of girlfriends that carried me when I couldn't put one foot in front of the other: Krissy, Kristy, Teanna, Lindsay, Toni, Megan, Charlotte, Linda, Erika, Jolene, Francis, Andrea, Kelly, Lindsey, Kim, Lauren, Kate, Ryan, and a host of others. Know that if you sent me an encouraging message, a text, a phone call, etc., you were my lifeline.

To my amazing cover designer, Madisen Mayfield and my editor, Jaclyn Reuter. You both do amazing work.

To my coach Sloane Kini who empowered me to stop talking about the book and start writing the book. I never would have reached the finish line without you.

To my favorite educators that pushed me and inspired me to be who I am today: Mr. Tom Downard, Ms. Vicki Newman, Ms. Judy Robinson, Dr. Linda Forrest, Dr. Robbie Steward.

To my fellow soldiers: for those of you who stood by me when I needed strength and support, thank you. For those that gave me the honor of serving with you and trusted me with your mental health as well as your darkest demons, I am humbled. Thank you for your service.

Last but not least, my Matthew. You aren't mentioned in this book because I didn't want this to be one of those, "My life was awful, but now I have my Prince Charming" books. You have been my rock, my cheerleader, my sender of too many almonds, and my biggest supporter. Thank you for all you do for me. From 1999 to now we have quite a story. I love you.

Resources

1-800-273-8255

National Suicide Crisis Hotline. You can also call 911 or go to your nearest emergency room.

www.psychologytoday.com

This is an excellent resource on various topics related to mental health. This website also has a "Find a Therapist" link that allows you to search by specialty, geographic location, style of therapy, etc.

www.apa.org

The American Psychological Association website offers a variety of resources for consumers. This website also features a "find a psychologist" search function.

www.emdria.org

The Eye Movement Desensitization and Reprocessing International Association offers information about EMDR (trauma treatment modality) and features a "find a therapist" search function.